Is it time to think again?

A TRAVEL-GUIDE FOR LIFE'S GREATEST QUEST

GRAEME EVANS

Is It Time to Think Again?
Published by Graeme Evans
New Zealand

ISBN 978-0-473-46527-8 (Softcover)
ISBN 978-0-473-46528-5 (ePUB)
ISBN 978-0-473-46529-2 (Kindle)

Editing: Sue Beguely

Production & Typesetting:
Andrew Killick
Castle Publishing Services
www.castlepublishing.co.nz

Cover design:
Paul Smith

Foreword

Surely we are all truth-seekers in our own way. There has to be a *why*. Humanity can't exist in a meaningless vacuum. Questions about origin, purpose and destiny simmer at the edge of our cognition. They are asked by many; and if not asked by some, probably only because the questions are too hard – answers inaccessible, or not provided by secular philosophy or present-day education systems.

Graeme Evans has found a way into the big questions, and has set forth a tour guide of discoveries that honest enquirers will find compelling.

Graeme and I met as 18-year-olds (decades ago). It was on a train, out of Auckland for Christchurch; we were young hopefuls at the start of our military careers. I learned early on that Graeme's ideas are worth listening to. His faculty for original thought is impressive, and his theses seem to bear an other-worldly wisdom. Over the years since then we've encouraged each other in our faith journeys.

One day, out of the blue, he told me he was writing a book reinvestigating the claims of Evolution and exploring the evidence for a Creator. This seemed outrageous because, not only had I not realised his deep interest in the subject, I was unaware that he harboured any aspirations of being a writer. Imagine my astonishment when I read the first draft of this fascinating book.

As an enquirer who had already pondered the big questions, and read on them widely, I was amazed at what Graeme had come up with. His *Is It Time to Think Again?* is not just a rehash of what others have written. It is replete with angles that will astonish the open enquirer and thrill the existing believer. It peels away the assumptions and underpinning beliefs of Evolutionary claims, allowing breath-taking possibilities to emerge. Graeme's honest critique of Evolution recognises the wonder – the true, underlying wonder – in the universe. As wonder rises, despair clears, faith soars.

Read this book, and see how it wobbles your worldview. Think of the life-changing implications. Yesterday had a purposeful beginning, today has purpose, tomorrow … will never be the same.

Recognise the truth that Graeme discovers here. Consider his roadmap, without assumption or preconception – or peer influence. All other truth and meaning may settle into place.

Ken Francis

We live in a world in which we are bombarded with information and opinions from every angle. We hear one view and then, before we can turn around, another perspective arises that is so different we wonder if it has come from some other planet. Every time the media releases a story we find ourselves wondering if it is 'fake news'. Could it just be someone pushing their own agenda, or is it true?

This book comes about as a result of Graeme Evans' desire to understand the big issues of life and, ultimately, life's purpose. His gifting and experience as a software engineer and analytical thinker has been put to good use. In a careful, thoughtful, meticulous way he has sought to consider every angle and possibility to discover truths that pass the tests of objectivity. Having undertaken that process he now wants to share his discoveries with everyone who has the desire to explore and understand.

Is It Time to Think Again? is a travel guide for anyone who wants to find purpose in life and be inspired on their journey. This is a book that can be read and given to friends and family with confidence.

John Massam

Contents

Visit **IsItTimeToThinkAgain.com** for more resources, including a 'Footnotes' page that includes links to the web pages mentioned in the footnotes of this book.

Introduction

In the busy blur that typifies life in the 21st century, it is not easy to slow down sufficiently to ponder the big picture. How often do we have time to contemplate that age-old, philosophical question, 'What is the meaning of life?' – or even grab a brief moment to smell a rose? When did we last walk among trees that were well established before our grandparents were born, and ponder the passing of the generations, and the passage of time itself? Do we reflect on deep issues like the origin of the cosmos, the marvels of the natural world, the capabilities of the human mind, and where human civilization is heading? How, and to what extent, do our reflections on these subjects affect how we live our everyday lives?

Most of us have written a will to arrange for the material things we will leave behind when we die. But is that *it*? What will happen to *us* at that point? Is the real me, who thinks and loves and laughs, just a product of chemicals and neurons? Or do brain and body provide an interface for another dimension to our being – our soul – enabling us to interact with the physical world? Is death 'The End' as atheists and materialists insist? Or is it a transition into another realm, like a full-term baby departing the womb for the world outside, or a sprouting seed shedding its outer casing as it transforms into something much bigger and better?

If the spiritual world exists, then it is the ultimate destination – and reality – for all of us. If it exists, does the spiritual world break through into the here and now of this material world? Does God exist? If so, who is 'he',[1] what is he like, and why did he create the universe? Is he deftly engineering events according to a vast master plan, crafted with unimaginable wisdom, with end goals beyond our conception? If God exists, has he revealed himself to humankind and, if so, how, and what has he communicated? How important is this to us?

There are endless questions. The most vital one is, 'If God exists, can we find our way home and connect personally with the one who made us?'

For most of us, simplistic pat answers are inadequate for these sorts of questions. You may have pondered a number of them already and found some answers. Therefore, this book does not presume to say new things, but rather may serve as a tool to pull together various thoughts, experiences, and values about truth in a structured way. Hopefully you will encounter many stimulating thoughts and fresh angles. Let it function as a 'travel guide' or 'road map' that helps you revisit and explore the big questions.

We don't usually study a map for hours on end. We use it to alert us to things in the vicinity that we might otherwise miss, to orient ourselves and understand what we see as we look around, or to find our way to a desired destination. Therefore, you might find it helpful to read this book differently from other books. Allow yourself to put it down and pursue a train of thought it has triggered, or research an aspect further. You may choose to read quickly through some sections which do not interest you, and more slowly through others on topics you need to consider more deeply.

Many people don't slow down enough to ponder life's big issues in significant depth, or don't consider them worthy of urgency.

---

1. The traditional convention of male pronouns will be used for the Creator and God throughout this book.

We are all free to avoid the big questions. But we can also regularly set aside time to think again, and to make that activity one of our main life quests, or even our life's greatest quest.

Telling Truth from Fiction

When we start on a thinking journey, we quickly realise that many sincere people hold conflicting philosophies and perspectives. Many individuals and groups hastily apply their own spin to objective realities, rather than seeing them as red flags challenging their thinking and beliefs. In many streams of contemporary thinking it is OK to create one's own subjective 'truth', with little regard for whether that truth will ultimately pass the test of time. Our post-modern, 21st century society makes a virtue of tolerating different views. This approach helps us all to live together amicably, but also sacrifices a degree of honesty. Some commentators claim that we are now living in the 'post-truth era'. This feature of contemporary society can be exacerbated by modern tools, such as social media, that tend to thicken the walls of people's personal echo-chambers. It seems we are all clever enough to deceive and delude ourselves, and to insulate ourselves within bubbles of our own perception.

The laws of science and the rules of basic arithmetic imply that objective truth does exist. Throughout this book, that sense of factual objectivity is the intended meaning when the word 'truth' is used on its own. But, in the muddied waters of our post-modern world, how can we reliably discern truth from fiction – or outright lies? This ability will be crucial throughout a journey like this. So, at its beginning, we need to review our experience and understanding of truth, and consider how we can best discern it.

Our 'fiction detectors' should sound an alarm whenever people dictate their own truth to us. Their assertions may not be true. They will certainly not be the whole truth; a convincing lie usually needs some half-truths to ensnare people. Real truth is objective. It will be proven by the test of time, regardless of what people may do with, or to, the person who spoke or wrote it. The truth of a proposition is not determined by the qualifications, status or reputation of the person who articulates it, although these might help others accept it more readily. Real truth will change and define *us*: it will cause recalibration if we are authentic in our response to it, or we will harden ourselves against it if we are not.

There is a deep partnership between truth and humility. An attitude of superiority towards others, or views that differ from our own, usually leads to self-deception. Superiority, hubris, and other forms of pride tend to dull our objectivity and blind us to wider realities. Further, the antithesis of humility is a self-serving presumption that projects its own perspective onto truth, and ultimately substitutes its own perception *for* truth.

There is also a deep partnership between truth and integrity. If we are unwilling to recalibrate ourselves according to what we discover then we will, even unconsciously, invent ways to twist or dismiss the truth, so that it does not challenge us. This propensity should not be underestimated because it comes naturally to all of us. Humility and integrity help us to recognise our errors when circumstances or situations expose them, and to embrace the recalibration that beckons at that point.

It can be difficult to verify that a claim is true, unless it is consistently supported by empirical observation, as with Newton's laws of motion. Observations that are consistent with a belief do not necessarily prove the belief is correct, because they can have valid, alternative explanations. In contrast, one single inconsistency is sufficient to show that a hypothesis is false. The method used by detectives to solve a crime illustrates this. They compile a list of possible suspects that fit the evidence to date. One single new piece of evidence may eliminate one or several suspects from that list. So, we should give considerable weight to any objective evidence that runs counter to a particular claim. We should also be alert to people who dismiss evidence that is inconvenient to their claims, or who are not willing to consider that something might be a red flag requiring a reassessment on their part.

We are all susceptible to a weakness in human perception where existing perspectives and expectations create filters that cause us to overlook things, which are obvious to others who employ different filters. Most of us have some funny stories that we can tell against ourselves in this regard. However, this weakness works against us in key areas that are not funny at all. It has been exploited by totalitarian governments to manipulate the masses. The norms of our own society create filters for us too; we may become aware of their existence only when unexpected events cause us loss and anguish, and give us the wisdom of hindsight. This weakness in perception is similar to what psychologists call *naïve realism.*[1] It also occurs when scientists collect and interpret their observations or data; they can miss relevant observations because they weren't looking for them. It can also colour their interpretations and conclusions – which are often already formed, if only tentatively – creating expectations and filters while they are in the field. Our perceptions and beliefs can easily blind us to other valid possibilities – and to flaws in our own thinking.

---

1. In social psychology, *naïve realism* is the human tendency to believe we see the world around us objectively, and that people who disagree with us must be uninformed, irrational or biased. (Wikipedia).

We should be cautious about 'expert' opinions, rather than overawed by them. In court cases, it is quite common for expert witnesses to be called who disagree directly with the expert opinions presented by opposing counsel. It is relatively easy to find an expert who says what we want to hear. While many highly-qualified physicists currently support the big bang theory, there is a significant number of equally qualified physicists who do not. The same is true of the theory of evolution. While the majority view often proves to be correct, the history of science contains a number of milestones where the prevailing view was overturned by new discoveries and paradigms. It is right to try to understand the majority views within the scientific community. However, we should also look out for those who have the conviction and courage to walk an unpopular road, rather than follow the pack down the easy highway of the majority view. Venturing into this territory requires healthy scepticism and discernment, as many crackpots and bull artists can also be found there. But in the commercial world, this territory is where we find the entrepreneurs. It is wise to seek and heed the advice of well-qualified people, and to obtain second opinions. However, we should not unquestioningly abdicate our own judgement to 'experts'.

It is easy to spot errors in what people say when they are 'on the other side of the fence from us' on any issue. However, it is more difficult to identify them in people on our side of the fence, who are saying what we want to hear. It is especially difficult to recognise errors in our own thinking, both as individuals and as a society. We are all guilty of hearing what we want to hear, and this is a tough tendency to overcome. In fact, we may be wise not to claim that we have 'arrived' in this regard. However, we are often unaware that the side of the fence where we find ourselves is usually a product of our upbringing, or norms we have absorbed uncritically, rather than having arrived at this position through careful, objective, and balanced deliberation. Consequently, Jonathan Swift's pithy warning may have some application for all of us: 'It is useless to attempt to reason a man out of a thing he was never reasoned into'.[2]

So, facts don't necessarily speak for themselves, because we always interpret them through our own philosophical framework, and are oblivious to flaws in our own framework. Further, because we usually share that framework with people who are important and dear to us, we are reluctant to question its truthfulness. It takes considerable courage and respect for truth to do this. For many people, the risk of incurring ire, losing important relationships, and finding themselves on their own, makes recalibration of their philosophical framework a bridge too far. If our existing framework is non-negotiable, then we invent ways to make challenging facts fit within it, instead of seeing them as 'red flags' to our thinking.

We should be aware that our starting assumptions will usually predetermine our conclusions, especially if we view those assumptions as infallible axioms and never revisit them. If our foundational assumptions are actually flawed, why should we expect our end conclusions to be any different? The layers of logic between our assumption and conclusions may be perfectly sound. If so, this will only deepen our self-deception. We are not, of ourselves, the fountain of truth. Each one of us has flaws in our thinking, which result from erroneous starting assumptions. Will Jonathan Swift's statement prove true of us: are aspects of our current thinking 'things that we were never reasoned into'? Breaking out of this state takes considerable respect for truth – and courage to swim against the flow.

---

2. Slightly paraphrased from the original: 1721, A Letter to a Young Gentleman, Lately Enter'd Into Holy Orders by a Person of Quality (Jonathan Swift), Second Edition, (Letter Dated January 9, 1720), Quote Page 27, Printed for J. Roberts at the Oxford Arms in Warwick Lane, London.

To have any hope of identifying real truth, we need to search for it with great humility and integrity, allowing it to change who and what we are. Further, we should proactively seek truth because we value these changes. It is healthy to read articles, and dialogue and debate with people with whom we disagree, as this can expose our faulty thinking. It can also open the door to valid ideas, angles, discoveries, and understanding that we have not previously considered. This ongoing attitude of humility and integrity should reduce the risk of our creating bubbles of misperception around ourselves; it should also gradually expose and pop ones that we, or others, have previously created.

There is a valuable question that we can ask ourselves in order to gauge our respect for truth and our openness to it, as well as the depth of our humility and integrity. It probes our openness to the possibility we may be wrong, and our willingness to embrace what we discover, so that it changes who and what we are. This question cuts through the confusing clutter of details and goes to the heart of any matter. It can be couched in the plural for a collective situation, or in the singular as a personal litmus test. The question is: If we are seriously mistaken in this issue, do we really want to know?[3] A variation on this can be applied as a double question to flush out flawed assumptions on any issue: What have we assumed? If these assumptions are incorrect, do we really want to know?

If we do not want to know, then we will find or invent ways to defend and justify our perceptions and thinking, because we want them to be true and need to convince ourselves that they are true. It is then very easy to fall into the trap of *circular reasoning* where

---

3. If this question is asked in a collective context with a culture that answers 'no, not really', then some further soul-searching questions arise: Should I bite my tongue and not make waves? Or, do I have a role to play in changing the culture? Is it time for me to move on?

flawed assumptions colour our understanding in ways that feed back to endorse those assumptions. While this principle is easy to understand, it is often difficult to identify in practice, especially when we are the ones doing it. Self-justification of this nature ultimately results in self-deception. The frightening reality is that we all have a tendency to do this.

Therefore, we must make every effort to eliminate attitudes, assumptions and prejudices that cloud or colour our thinking, and prevent us from considering sensible possibilities outside our current perspective and world view. How will we respond to discoveries that are different from what we have always previously thought? How will we respond to discoveries that are not what we *want* them to be? Does our commitment to truth also commit us to proactively seeking out and embracing such discoveries, letting them change our perspective – and consequently shape who we are?

The search for truth is a journey of discovery that will last our whole lives. If our search is authentic, it will touch, change or tweak every aspect of our thinking and perspective. Over time, it will transform our personal goals and priorities, making us much less self-centred. It will help us to see through the marketing hype and other hoopla that characterises 21st century life, and enable us to discern twisted norms and values pervading modern society. It will also calibrate our fiction-detectors and increase their sensitivity, thereby helping us to recognise fiction when it is presented as fact.

Gradually, we learn to recognise times when we need to rethink our stance on a particular issue. Our quest to discover and embrace truth is characterised by a continual willingness to humbly ask the question: Is it time to think again?

PART ONE

Thinking Again: About Our Origins

Origins

It is sensible to start at the beginning. Our perception of origins is hugely important because it determines our answer to the bedrock question, 'What is the meaning of life?' Our answer, in turn, dramatically impacts our identity and direction, both as individuals and as a society.

We need to build on a foundational assumption that life is not some narcissistic dream with just 'me' in it, but that this world is real, with billions of wonderfully complex and creative people. How did this real universe come to be here, with all its consistent physical laws that make it work? How did life get started on this planet? Is this vast universe, and the wonderfully complex and diverse biosphere that we inhabit, merely the product of chance and the 'arbitrary' laws of physics and chemistry, as atheistic philosophy dictates? Or was it created by a super-intelligent, super-energetic being who exists in dimensions beyond this space-time universe?[1] Does life have purpose, even a deep and significant purpose? Or does it have no meaning at all beyond passing on our genes – hopefully without too many mutations – to the next generation?

In any professional field, and in many aspects of life, there are

1. There will be much more to the creator than is apparent from what we observe, just as there is more to us than people can perceive from examining something we have made.

grey areas where the real truth may not be obvious to us. If there is significant evidence a particular perspective or line of thinking may have some truth to it, then rejecting that possibility because we don't like it, is a recipe for error and stupidity. This is especially so if we then embark on a one-sided, highly selective crusade to prove to ourselves that our view is right, and the other view is not. Such an approach to the subject of origins, which is particularly susceptible to one's interpretation of various facts, will be a recipe for much folly.

The atheistic philosophy and assumptions incumbent within modern academia assert that God does not exist and that this universe, life and the biosphere came about all by themselves without any intelligent, external first-cause or subsequent involvement. The alternative is axiomatically rejected, and often scoffed out of the room. Time itself will eventually have the final say. However, you and I cannot wait that long because we have only one life to live, and it is scarily short. There are a few well-qualified scientists who disagree with important aspects of the current status quo, and some of them have paid a high price for their disagreement. Yet many of the conclusions they have come to through their intellectual honesty are fascinating and thought-provoking. There is a growing mountain of scientific observations that challenge many atheistic assumptions. In our roadmap, we need to explore some of the bigger inconveniences – and outright contradictions – in this regard, familiarise ourselves with them, and perhaps even deprogramme ourselves where necessary. The first half of this book should help you do that.

A discussion of origins will be necessarily technical in places. Brief explanations of a few terms are provided as footnotes. However, it is not practical to explain every term.[2] This topic occupies almost

---

2. If you encounter a technical term that is unfamiliar, typing it into a search engine should not only furnish a good definition, but may also offer an interesting side-excursion at that point of our travel-guide.

the first half of the book. The material is treated in depth because most people have been bombarded exclusively with atheistic interpretations and perspectives all their lives, and have unquestioningly taken them on board as truth. Readers in this category will hopefully find this part of the book interesting, perhaps even essential, in facilitating a more balanced view that allows the second half of this book to be read in an objective manner. This first half tries to summarise many recent scientific discoveries that are inconvenient to the atheistic evolutionary story. This may stimulate further study into some of these topics, especially if this discussion is too condensed for your taste.[3]

However, for most people, it would be sensible to start at the beginning, and build on what we already know from observing the world around us. Are there any signposts within our current knowledge and experience that will provide reliable orientation? Hopefully, this discussion on origins will help readers to think again about that huge and important subject.

3. If you have not bought into the atheistic world view, and scientific things don't 'ring your bell', then you might speed-read through it, read just the concluding sections, or jump straight to the section titled Consciousness. This book is a road map to use as you see fit.

The Universe

Early last century, scientists finally started to grasp the sheer size of the cosmos – that there are probably as many galaxies as there are stars in our own Milky Way galaxy – more than two hundred billion! Various probes over the last fifty years have revealed tremendous diversity everywhere we look within our own solar system. Every discovery seems to lift the lid on a host of new questions. What are we to make of all these fascinating new discoveries? We are learning mostly about the *what* and *where* of the cosmos, but concrete observations of the *how*, *when* and *why* are more elusive.

Thermodynamics and Expansion

The second law of thermodynamics tells us that the universe cannot be infinitely old. If it was, it would have experienced *heat death* aeons ago. The expansion of the universe also supports its having a beginning. Observations suggest that the very 'fabric' of space seems to be expanding and accelerating,[1] which suggests that even

1. If you are not familiar with this terminology and its associated concepts, use the phrases 'metric expansion of space' and 'fabric of space expanding accelerating' in a search engine. There are several astronomy and physics websites that give good explanations. en.wikipedia.org/wiki/Accelerating_expansion_of_the_universe is also useful.

the dimensions of space had a beginning. So, atheists and creationists all tend to agree that the universe had a finite beginning, but are poles apart as to the nature and cause of that beginning.

The first law of thermodynamics says that matter and energy may change form (or convert as per $E=mc^2$), but are never gained or lost (created or destroyed). This raises the obvious question: if there is no natural process that can cause a gain in matter and energy, what was the source of the vast quantity of matter and energy that exists in the known universe – which enabled its beginning?

Many atheists plead for string theory – or a variant, M-theory – as providing a possible source. However, string theory is not a theory in the scientific sense because, conspicuously, there is no experimental evidence to validate it. String theory would still have a heat-death problem if strings have always existed from infinity past, or a causation problem if they had a finite origin. That is, it would merely create a new set of problems rather than solve the root dilemma. And it cannot explain the beginning of the dimensions of space itself. So those who advocate string theory as the first-cause of the universe have in essence turned their backs on experimental science, and embraced a whimsical hypothesis that is not supported by direct scientific observation – nor logical reasoning, such as the principle of Occam's razor.[2]

This all strongly suggests that this universe was caused by something or someone that is outside the system. The atheist-dominated scientific establishment rejects such a possibility by axiom: only purely naturalistic explanations are acceptable, because you cannot put God in a test-tube and observe him directly. However, this is a double standard, because you cannot put atheistic philosophy

2. Occam's razor: the principle (attributed to William of Occam 1285-1349 AD – also spelled Ockham) that, among competing hypotheses, the simplest one (with the fewest assumptions) should be selected.

into a test-tube either. How wise is it to completely ban a serious possibility from the table, when there is a lot of indirect evidence to support it, especially when our repository of scientific observations provides no mechanism for the universe to have come into existence by itself, without any need for an external 'original cause'?

At first glance, the expansion of the universe seems consistent with big bang theory, which is formally described within astrophysics as the Standard Cosmological Model (SCM). The big bang can correctly be called a theory, because there are many scientific observations that are consistent with it. However, we should not ignore the reality that this theory has a number of serious mathematical problems, and is inconsistent with other observations. It requires several significant hypothetical *fudge factors* such as inflation and vast quantities[3] of dark matter and dark energy, just to keep it tenable. While several astronomical phenomena are likely to be caused by black holes, there is no evidence that the necessary quantities of dark matter and energy actually exist. However, they are essential for the big bang to retain any credibility. These problems were identified in *An Open Letter to the Scientific Community* written by 34 top cosmological scientists and published in *New Scientist* on 22 May 2004. The letter was subsequently endorsed by several hundred other professional scientists, engineers, and independent researchers. Up until 2014 it was accessible on a dedicated website[4] but from January 2015 this site seems to have been deactivated.

One of the difficulties for big bang theorists is to explain how

---

3. Approximately 24 times more than the quantity of visible matter and energy.
4. A Google search for 'cosmology statement open letter 2004' will find the letter as there are plenty of creationist sites that are keen to keep publishing it, even though the original signatories were not creationists. It is also published on this book's website: IsItTimeToThinkAgain.com.

and why the large-scale structure of the universe formed at all amid a random explosion. Currently, the most popular hypothesis to solve this problem is 'inflation'.[5] Inflation hypothesises that the initial universe somehow accelerated and expanded at zillions of times faster than the speed of light, contrary to Einstein's theory of General Relativity. It is also hypothesised that the early cosmic material was able to accelerate and expand like this, because it somehow had zero mass – and had not yet formed into protons, neutrons, and electrons. The question must then be asked: Is there any observational evidence that $E=mc^2$ works both ways, so that pure energy can turn into protons, neutrons, and electrons? Or is this merely a philosophical assertion?[6]

The inflation hypothesis goes on to claim that the early universe somehow then decelerated to the expansion rate that we now observe. But this creates a further problem: How could that inflation have been so *flat*? In other words, how could such a super-explosion have ended up with the universe being so stable and consistent with our current observations? As one author recently wrote: 'Inflation was Alan Guth's attempt to explain why the early

---

5. A number of cosmologists claim that inflation also solves several other serious problems for the big bang, namely horizon, flatness and magnetic-monopole.
6. An exciting physics experiment is currently being developed to validate Breit and Wheeler's 1934 theory that two photons can convert into an electron and positron. It will be interesting to see how they get two photons to react together, rather than simply pass through each other. Even if this experiment is successful, the synthesis of protons and neutrons from pure energy will remain a more difficult experimental challenge. Success in this too would definitely allow big bang proponents to legitimately claim that it is supported by some hands-on experimental results (i.e. real science), rather than mere hypothesising about unobserved past events, in order to fit the data that we collect today into a purely naturalistic framework.

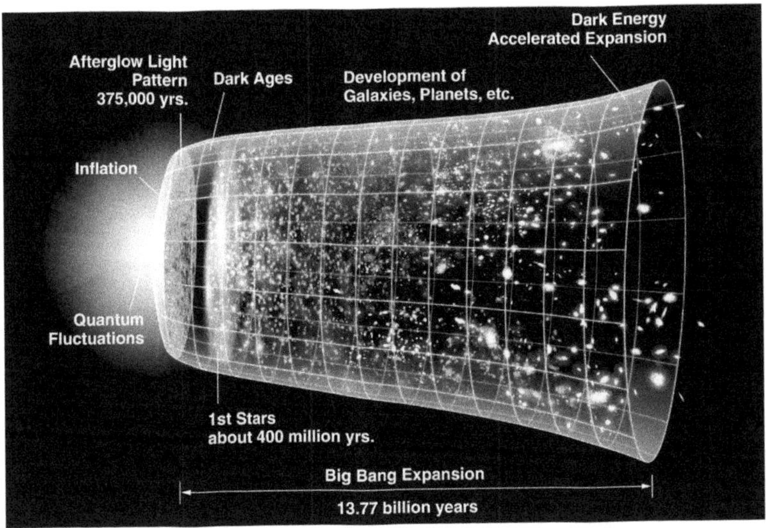

Figure 1. Big Bang Expansion (illustrating 'inflation' at the start).

universe after the Big Bang was so very 'flat', which is to say, why the force of the explosion matched the force of gravity to one part in 10^{60}. To put this in perspective, there are about 10^{80} protons in the visible universe. So, 10^{20} protons, about one grain of sand, would have unbalanced the Big Bang, causing it either to re-collapse into a black hole, or to expand so fast as to never form stars and galaxies. One grain of sand more, one grain less, and we would not be here.'[7] (This is a significant 'fine tuning' problem which will be addressed in the next section.)

---

7. Sheldon, R. (2014, March). Bang for the buck: What the BICEP2 consortium's discovery means. *Evolution News and Science Today*. Retrieved from evolutionnews.org/2014/03/bang_for_the_bu/.

Figure 2. Hubble Ultra Deep Field Image (NASA). These are all galaxies (about 10,000 of them), not stars, and this is a very small portion of the sky (about one percent of the area covered by the full moon).

When the Hubble Deep Field pictures of the farthest reaches of the known universe were being planned, cosmologists were eager to see what matter looked like close to its primordial state, as it was in the very early stages of the big bang – the light having taken that long to reach us. To the researchers' amazement, when the images came in, they showed perfectly formed galaxies just like the ones very close to us, including spectra that indicated the presence of heavier metals[8] which should not exist in very young galaxies if the Standard Cosmological Model (SCM) is correct. Infrared imagery from other telescopes, such as Spitzer, has corroborated the existence of heavier metals in very distant galaxies, and revealed distant galaxies a thousand times more massive than our own Milky Way. The very existence of such huge galaxies at that distance also raises fundamental questions about the SCM, since it did not predict that matter could concentrate that quickly after the big bang. Atheistic cosmologists gave a small cough to clear their throats, rapidly concluded and agreed among themselves that 'galaxies must somehow form much faster than we had thought', and raced off to tweak their mathematical models so they would accommodate the new discoveries. Once again, a serious possibility was banned from the table – that galaxies have always been galaxies because their matter and energy came into existence (or was created) as mature galactic structures that included heavier metals. Multiple mini-creations of each galaxy in a mature and stable universe are rejected outright by atheistic dogma because instant structure suggests an intelligent architect. However, one single big bang event is somehow perfectly acceptable, even though it is not supported by the Deep Field images and Spitzer data. In addition, it has the problems identified in the *Open Letter to the Scientific Community*, and needs extraordinarily accurate and Einstein-defying inflation, with unknown mechanisms for its start and finish. While many cosmologists believe that inflation also solves the flatness and horizon problems, and that it explains several observations that would otherwise be problematic for the

8. In astronomy, the term 'metal' means all elements higher in the periodic table than Helium. In the SCM these should not form until very late in the life of the first stars, after all their hydrogen has been used up, that is several billion years after they compressed sufficiently under their own gravity to ignite their hydrogen nuclear fusion reactions.

big bang, this does not prove that inflation or the big bang actually took place. Nor does it prove that we observe only four percent of the universe because the other 96 percent is made of the unobservable hypothetical fudge factors of dark matter and dark energy.

In a quest for a purely materialistic explanation of origins, atheistic cosmologists have created terms such as *vacuum bubble*, *quantum fluctuations* and *metastable false vacuum*, and devised various mathematical formulas such as the Wheeler-DeWitt equation. This equation assumes that the total matter and energy content of the universe is zero, which seems contrived and even nonsense to many people. Antimatter certainly exists if only briefly in target areas of particle accelerators. But this isn't *negative matter*. Nor is negative energy the same as hypothetical dark energy. If matter and antimatter collide, they annihilate each other and release a huge amount of energy as per $E=mc^2$. The Wheeler-DeWitt equation claims that negative matter and negative energy *have* to exist to negate all the matter and energy that we clearly observe. This acknowledges a reality: if the total matter and energy in the universe is not zero, then the first law of thermodynamics requires a source for it. Atheistic philosophy would have no answer to this problem, and could not even cross the starting-line. However, scientific *observation* suggests very strongly that the total matter and energy content of the universe has a vast positive value, and that negative matter and negative energy do not exist.

Some of the SCM mathematics can accommodate observations about cosmic microwave background (CMB) radiation and the abundance of hydrogen in the cosmos. The theorists appeal to these as supporting their claims, while at the same time ignoring the many observations that create difficulties. Remember that supporting facts can turn out to have valid alternative explanations, and that a single inconsistency is often sufficient proof that a claim is not true.

Based largely on work by the late UK physicist, Stephen Hawking, many atheistic cosmologists hypothesise that the universe pre-existed the big bang as a 'singularity', that is, a point with no size at all. While this appears to solve the cause of the big bang, it immediately creates three new problems. Firstly, the current laws of physics would have broken down in such a singularity. It is therefore impossible to conduct scientific experiments to test the laws of physics in a singularity, which makes the hypothesis unscientific by definition. Secondly, how could such a singularity come into existence in the first place? Thirdly, what triggered the change and how could a singularity then transform itself into the universe we observe today? Thus, it seems that the efforts of atheistic cosmologists are pure philosophising, with fundamental flaws in their starting assumptions. Violating the principle of Occam's razor and first law of thermodynamics are only two of these flaws. Given the need for so many unobserved fudge factors, it also seems that there is very little hard experimental or observational scientific evidence to confirm that their starting assumptions, ensuing thinking, and mathematical models have much in common with the real origin and history of the cosmos.

There is another less obvious but very significant problem with the big bang out of nothing story. The big bang requires, and is completely dependent on, the laws of physics. These immutable laws of physics are completely consistent, and are foundational to a functional universe. Where did they come from, and how could they have been established within a purely atheistic framework? Having grown up with them, we take the laws of physics and chemistry for granted. However, is it reasonable to claim that purely random, mindless processes could devise and implement all the complex, consistent, and mutually interacting laws essential for a functional universe and diverse biosphere? Is the phrase *random laws* an oxymoron? How could random laws be consistent throughout the earth and cosmos? We will explore these questions in greater depth later, in the section on 'Scientific Laws'.

The conundrum for the purely naturalistic big bang is so simple that a five-year-old could understand it. How could there be absolutely nothing – perhaps not even the dimensions of space or the laws of physics themselves – one nanosecond before the big bang event, and absolutely everything in the current universe one nanosecond after it? And how could this be achieved through self-contained natural processes that do not violate the first law of thermodynamics – assuming that the laws of physics somehow came into existence before the big bang could start?

In our road map these questions need to be seriously considered: Why is there something instead of nothing?[9] How could our universe create itself – including all its own laws of physics and chemistry, dimensions, matter, and energy – from nothing, without outside help? Are the incumbent atheistic claims and hypothetical models within our scientific establishment sensible, or are they a chimera? On the other hand, is the cosmos full of signposts that point to its having been created through the volition of some vastly energetic, intelligent, and capable source that is outside the system?

Fine Tuning

This is a sensible point in our travel guide to explore the 'fine tuning of the universe' and its implications. Physicists have identified

---

9. We can – and should – also ponder the corollary question: Why does God exist, rather than nothing at all? There is an important distinction between the two questions. We do not see and understand much at all about the spiritual world, and are therefore unable to make significant progress with the second question – on this side of death, anyway. However, we can observe the physical universe very objectively. The scientific laws of thermodynamics and our experience with complex systems both have profound implications – if we are willing to let them calibrate our thinking.

more than thirty physical constants in the universe, such as the speed of light, that have arbitrary values. They are what they are with no mathematical or scientific reason, unlike the mathematical constants π and e. Many of these arbitrary values seem to be very finely tuned, some to 20 or more decimal places. If any one of these was just a little different, then the basic chemistry of life would be impossible, or our sun could not sustain a hospitable environment for our biosphere. The probability that all of them have their finely tuned values by mere chance is mind-blowingly small, akin to winning a lottery drawn from all the electrons in the universe instead of a barrel of marbles, not just once, but several times in a row. The implications of this are fairly obvious.

Atheistic theorists acknowledge this problem, but 'solve' it by asserting that we are living in just one of a vast number of parallel universes – the multiverse hypothesis. Our universe just happens to be one where the constants, and the other laws of physics and chemistry, are conducive to life – which they believe will arise all by itself in favourable conditions. Further, they claim our universe merely has the right random permutation of physical constants and laws, otherwise we wouldn't be here to observe it. This is of course pure speculation, because we will never be able to scientifically observe other universes. Also, the logic of this position is fundamentally flawed because, while they believe it accounts for the colossal coincidences we observe, it does not adequately explain how and why the universe – or multiverse – exists, rather than nothing at all. Even if we fully understood all the physical laws of our own universe, this would be no help whatsoever to understanding the origin of the multiverse, because all other universes would have different physics from our own. It also raises the obvious question: if we can't explain how our own universe came into existence through purely naturalistic processes, how can we sensibly claim that a vast or even infinite number of parallel universes – which we cannot observe – came into existence through purely natural processes that were different from ours? While random permutations of physical constants might be a slightly plausible concept, the questions raised in the previous section as to the rationality of *random laws* are equally applicable to a multiverse.

The multiverse hypothesis completely defies the principle of Ockham's razor. We should also ask whether it is reasonable to postulate a multiverse (something that we have not observed, and can *never* observe scientifically) but dictate that a different explanation (a creator God) is unacceptable because we cannot observe God directly using scientific instruments. This is especially so when a rational case can be made for an intelligent creator when (unlike the multiverse) there are many scientific observations that are consistent with the teleological argument[10] and provide considerable indirect, supporting evidence.

Our Own Solar System

Many observations of our own solar system seem inconsistent with a purely naturalistic explanation of its origin. The sun and planets all rotate in the same direction – which is consistent with the reigning nebular hypothesis. However, if our sun was formed when a swirling cloud of gas and dust collapsed in on itself, then the law of conservation of angular momentum[11] says it should be spinning five to ten times more rapidly than its current average rate.[12] This law works consistently for both ice-skaters and stellar

10. The argument for the existence of God from the evidence of order, and hence design, in nature.
11. This law is the reason why an ice-skater spins more rapidly when she pulls her arms and legs into as small a radius as possible.
12. The Sun rotates faster (26 days) at its equator than at the poles (36 days).

bodies. In the extreme, the collapsed mass after a supernova forms a pulsar that can rotate at more than 30 times per second. The *angular momentum* would have prevented the primordial sun from collapsing sufficiently into a core with conditions that could light the fire of nuclear fusion. This creates a similar difficulty for the naturalistic formation of other stars – especially those with planets. Cosmologists have suggested several mechanisms that might have shed the missing angular momentum for our sun, but none of these is without problems.

The sun's axis of rotation is tilted more than seven degrees from the ecliptic.[13] This phenomenon, and the tilt of the rotation axis of the earth and other planets, are seriously inconsistent with the nebular hypothesis. Cosmologists usually resort to hypothetical high-mass impacts as a mechanism to account for all these tilts. This explanation stretches credibility at a statistical level. More importantly, it is inconsistent with the near planar and circular orbital paths we observe.

Like the biosphere, our solar system is full of diversity, and we observe many things that still defy naturalistic explanation. There are serious inconsistencies with our best prevailing theories and postulations. For example, the accretion theory is the reigning hypothesis for the creation of the planets. Computer models can successfully simulate the hypothetical formation of inner rocky planets,[14] but not the outer gas giants. There are also significant problems with its foundational mechanisms for transforming extremely thin *star dust* – with a density less than one puff of cigarette smoke dispersed

---

13. The ecliptic refers to the plane of orbit of Earth and the other planets.
14. There are problems even with the simulations for the inner planets. None have been able to produce a result that matches the observed sizes and orbits of Mercury, Venus, Earth, Mars, and the asteroids. See www.nature.com/articles/nature16322.

in a large theatre – into asteroid-sized planetesimals large enough to generate their own weak gravitational fields. However, accretion computer models all simply assume this, and are initialised with various distributions of planetesimals as their starting point.

Like the fine-tuning of the universe, our earth has more than 100 *Goldilocks factors*[15] that are all essential to support intelligent life. They include: a stable single star (most stars are in binary systems), near-circular orbit at an optimum distance for liquid water, optimal planet size, chemical composition (sufficient and widely distributed nutrients, but no major toxicity), density of the atmosphere (including critical levels of greenhouse gases), sufficient water and a weather system, rotational speed, axial tilt (seasons expand the habitable latitudes, as well as providing other benefits), sufficient magnetic field, ozone layer, single large moon, large outer planet such as Jupiter, position in the galaxy, and type of galaxy. We can reasonably expect further research in several fields to steadily identify more factors. When the low probabilities of each of these factors are multiplied, the combined improbability of them *all* coming together in one planet is considerably less than one in the number of stars in the entire universe. The design implications of this improbability are fairly compelling.

Conclusion

We live in privileged times. None of the generations that lived earlier than the last eighty years had any inkling of the sheer size of the universe. However, along with these recent discoveries have come many observations that are inconvenient for the atheistic and materialistic philosophy that pervades academic communities and our

15. Goldilocks factors: not too big or small, not too hot or cold... but just right.

post-Christian society. We need to embrace these problems with intellectual honesty and integrity, and think through their ramifications, even if they are seriously uncomfortable, or not what we would like them to be. It would seem that academia has created its own echo chamber, where only the Standard Cosmological Model is permitted. However, the scientific laws of thermodynamics and probability, and science's many observations of the earth, solar system and cosmos, provide objective benchmarks against which the credibility of various philosophical claims about the origins of the universe can be assessed. Did the universe create itself without outside help, or was it created? If it was created, what might the universe tell us about its creator?

Life and Biosphere:

The Origin of Life

While the cosmos is complex and defies some of the laws of probability, the chemistry of life and deft interplay of multiple symbiotic relationships in the biosphere are in a bigger league of complexity altogether. Many advocates of the prevailing evolutionary paradigm tend to downplay the complexities and improbabilities involved, or simply ignore many significant problems. However, over the last half-century, discoveries about cellular nanotechnology, embryonic development, metabolic control mechanisms, immune systems, the brain, and the sheer volume of information contained in DNA have accumulated into a significant mountain of complexity that is increasingly difficult to explain within a purely naturalistic paradigm.

In a documentary I watched on TV a few years ago, a scientist acknowledged these problems and stated that we don't understand the solution to them at present. However, he went on to say, 'But we know that evolution is true, and that one day we will have the ability to understand the details of how it actually worked to produce the results that we observe.' It was a statement of belief, not one of proven fact. I offer a statement of my own, with which all parties should be able to agree, if only reluctantly: 'Either Darwin's theory of evolution is an amazing and brilliant insight, or it is the biggest bungle in the history of science.' When you think it through, it can only be one or the other – there is no third option.

Early in our roadmap, we need to examine at least some of the big boulders in this growing mountain of complexity, and apply tests of 'truth or fiction' to competing claims within the associated debate. The issues identified in the following sections by no means comprise an exhaustive list. The aim is to present these in a sufficiently non-technical way that enables readers to understand easily, and also gain a good feel for the breadth of the debate itself.

The Primordial Soup

Three and a half billion years ago, according to the modern scientific consensus, all the raw chemical ingredients for life somehow accumulated somewhere on Earth in sufficient concentrations, and randomly assembled themselves into the first living cell. Is it even possible for such a chemical soup to form at all, or is this claim a myth? Whether a living cell could spontaneously form within such a soup is a topic for the next section. The immediate question is whether real scientific observations support or invalidate the claim that this hypothetical soup could actually form in the first place.

The primordial soup hypothesis states that some convenient volcano somewhere might have supplied all the common and trace minerals necessary for the chemistry of life. Further, before too many of these fresh, raw chemicals reacted with each other in ways that would destroy them or create other compounds toxic to life, several flashes of lightning, or perhaps UV light from the sun, provided the necessary extra energy for numerous amino acids to form. Then, before these reacted adversely with other compounds, they randomly combined to form the raw components of life – proteins and sugars – which, in turn, randomly arranged themselves into the first living cell.

There are two opposing camps with different ideas of the site of a primordial soup: one favours a volcanic vent in the ocean, and the other argues for a special pond somewhere. The following brief overview will give you a sense of the respective dilemmas:

- The most important problem for the pond camp is that the chemical reactions creating amino acids also create significantly greater quantities of tars and other compounds that are toxic to life, because they react adversely with amino acids and destroy them. In their famous experiment in 1952, Miller and Urey used special laboratory equipment to separate the amino acids from the toxic byproducts. In a pond there is no obvious mechanism to keep the valuable amino acids separate from these harmful byproducts.
- A volcanic vent in the ocean would overcome this problem, because the harmful byproducts would dissolve in the ocean and be carried away from the scene. However, so too would the amino acids. This would occur so rapidly they could never gather in sufficient concentrations to have even a remote chance of forming a cell.

While a few very specialised bacteria can thrive near some conducive volcanic vents, they all have unique repair systems that enable them to survive the increased rate of biochemical breakdown that occurs at these temperatures – that will kill all other bacteria. The need for 'super-repair' systems would significantly increase the complexity – and thereby the improbability – required for a viable first cell in this environment. The cooler temperature of a pond somewhere on the side of a volcano has a lot more going for it in this regard. Such is the nature of things – full of compromises.

Whether amino acids could form at all from lightning in the atmosphere is highly doubtful. Miller and Urey had to exclude oxygen completely from the gaseous mixture in their experiment, because it inhibits the formation of amino acids. This reality compels atheistic theorists to postulate some interesting scenarios for Earth's early atmosphere, and to postulate additional mechanisms which might have then changed the atmosphere into what we have today. Unfortunately, there is mounting evidence that oxygen has always been present in the earth's atmosphere. Also, the necessary percentages of hydrogen and ammonia could never have existed for millions of years in the atmosphere of a primordial Earth.[1] In addition, there is a Catch-22 with ammonia: while fairly high concentrations are necessary for the synthesis of amino acids, it is lethal to life even at much lower concentrations.[2]

Miller and Urey achieved only very low yields – less than two percent – of a few amino acids.[3] However, these low yields were achieved only because the products were artificially removed from the reaction location, preventing equilibrium (which would have stopped their production) and other reactions that would destroy them. Miller engaged in further work in this field over the remainder of his academic career. Recent analysis of some of the samples he kept, revealed that minute traces of most of the other 20 amino acids found in life were also produced – along with others not used in the chemistry of life. Over the subsequent decades, many researchers have explored other mechanisms for abiotic synthesis of amino acids, including the use of ultraviolet light and heat. They have been able to synthesise more significant yields – still only one

---

1. In those conditions molecular hydrogen would escape into space, and ammonia would be absorbed into the oceans where its presence would still be detectable today.
2. Ammonia is highly soluble in water. Most bacteria are completely inhibited by a concentration of 10 grams per litre – or approximately one percent. Only two milligrams per litre (0.0002%) is lethal to all fish.
3. Primarily these were glycine and alanine – the two simplest ones.

percent to two percent – of about ten of the amino acids that are used in the chemistry of life. The other ten amino acids require much more complex synthesis conditions to achieve significant yields, and it is difficult to conceive how this could have occurred in a purely natural pre-life environment. Even if two percent yields of all 20 amino acids could be achieved without their being subsequently destroyed in a primordial soup, how could such low concentrations provide a sufficient starting point for the spontaneous assembly of the first cell?

But, even if sufficient concentrations of all twenty could form spontaneously in a primordial soup, amino acids are only basic building blocks. They need to polymerise into long protein molecules of about 400 amino acids. Polymerisation is an equilibrium reaction, which is not favoured thermodynamically. Unfortunately, the presence of water creates big problems, because water tends to break down peptide bonds[4] faster than they form. It is very unlikely that a chain will spontaneously grow to more than 10 amino acids long. In the cell, this problem is overcome by cellular machines – which are also built with full-length protein molecules, which were synthesised by the cell itself or its parent. Various sugars are required in the chemistry of life as well, and these tend to react adversely with free amino acids and polypeptides. The nanomachinery within a living cell not only builds the long polypeptide chains of protein molecules, but prevents adverse reactions during that process. There are no such mechanisms within the hypothetical primordial soup.

Even if full-length protein chains could form, this also would not be sufficient. Proteins are useful only when they are correctly

---

4. A peptide bond is a chemical bond formed between two molecules when the carboxyl group of one molecule reacts with the amino group of the other molecule, releasing a molecule of water. Retrieved from www.sciencedaily.com/terms/peptide_bond.htm

folded in three dimensions, and would create a lot of mischief for a cell if they were folded incorrectly. From the 1950s to 1980s it was thought that proteins would spontaneously fold correctly. However, in the 1990s it was discovered that proteins will almost always fold incorrectly if left to their own devices. Within a living cell, a whole suite of special proteins called *molecular chaperones* perform the task of preventing newly manufactured proteins from folding incorrectly. They are then processed by another class of molecular machines called *chaperonins*, which perform the actual folding function, using energy supplied by ATP.[5] Molecular chaperones and chaperonins are themselves composed of correctly folded proteins. This creates a chicken-or-egg difficulty for the purely naturalistic view. So, the inconvenient realities of protein folding generate yet another fundamental problem for the primordial soup hypothesis.

The need for correctly folded proteins should not be underestimated. Most of the proteins in life are enzymes which increase the rate of their respective chemical reactions many millions of times. Without them, the chemistry of life just would not work. Because they are so crucial, if any one of them was missing, or was at too low a concentration, a hypothetical first cell would not be viable. No researcher has yet demonstrated how even one enzyme could have formed, and folded correctly, in a prebiotic solution. Nevertheless, the first cell would require hundreds of different specific enzymes, and hundreds of thousands of identical copies of each of them. If the primordial soup site – whether pond or ocean – is claimed to have had the same chemical composition as the first cell's cytoplasm, how could it have synthesised such vast numbers of these chemical wonders?

---

5. ATP is a special molecule that provides the energy that powers all cellular machines. It is itself synthesised by a special cellular machine called ATP synthase.

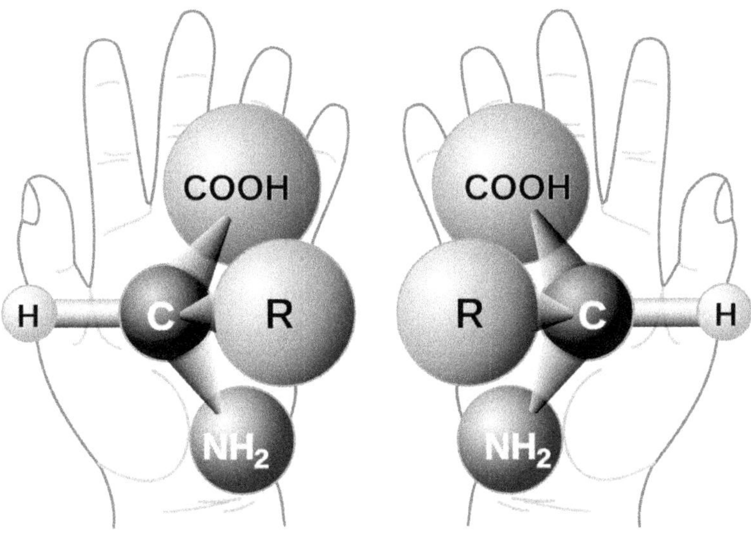

Figure 3. Amino acid chirality.

If that were not enough, there is the *amino acid chirality* problem. Amino acids come in two symmetrical forms, called left-handed and right-handed. The formation of amino acids by electric discharge, UV light, and heat all result in mixtures that are racemic, that is 50-50 left- and right-handed. However, all of life's chemistry has exclusively left-handed amino acids. The presence of even just a few right-handed amino acids would cause proteins to fold quite differently, which would destroy their function as enzymes. The probability of even a small protein with purely 250 left-handed amino acids forming in a 50-50 mixture is the same as flipping a coin and it coming up heads 250 times in a row. This probability is about the same as winning a lottery drawn from all the electrons in the known universe.

But we don't need just one small protein. The first cell would need millions[6] of pure left-handed protein chains averaging 400 amino acids each – not 250. All these 'pure-breeds' would need to find one another in a soup with trillions of 'mongrels', with no natural mechanism to help them do this.[7] The probability of one million pure-breeds averaging 400 amino acids long all being synthesised adjacent to each other in a 50-50 mixture is the same as winning a lottery drawn from all the electrons in the universe, not just once, but more than one million times *in a row*.

In the history of the many national lotteries that are run weekly all around the world, has anyone ever won the major prize even twice in row? There have been several very rare occurrences where a person or syndicate has won a major lottery a second time. But these wins were several years apart, and they had bought many tickets over the years between wins. No one has ever won a major lottery on consecutive weeks. Winning a lottery drawn from all the electrons in the universe just once would equate to winning a national mega lottery more than ten straight consecutive weeks by purchasing only a single ticket each week. Is this starting to give definition to the improbabilities involved in getting millions of pure left-handed proteins together all at once? If somebody won a national lottery twice in a row many people would be calling for an independent investigation to discover how it was rigged. Yet the improbability of synthesising enough exclusively left-handed amino acids for merely one million proteins would be the same as winning a weekly mega lottery consecutively for more than 200,000 years by purchasing a

6. An E.coli cell has about three million protein molecules. A budding yeast cell has 90 to 140 million. book.bionumbers.org/how-many-proteins-are-in-a-cell/.
7. Random molecular motion, in a liquid, irreversibly mixes and dilutes non-reacting chemicals very quickly – ensuring that any (highly improbable) pure-breeds will never find each other.

single ticket every week. If the relatively small improbability of two consecutive wins would cause many people to conclude outside interference of some sort had taken place, why does our academic community not draw a similar conclusion when confronted with astronomically greater improbabilities? Is it because their atheistic assumptions create a strong belief that there must have been a purely naturalistic first-cause mechanism (they just haven't found it yet), and this *belief* precludes all other possibilities?

Hopefully this section has given an idea of the extent of the many significant problems for those who wish to demonstrate the plausibility of a primordial soup, which is still the reigning 'scientific' hypothesis for the origin of life on Earth. There are many highly skilled scientists who would love to produce a breakthrough, by creating a plausible primordial soup in the laboratory. Despite considerable effort over 150 years, no one has done so, because the basic laws of chemistry do not cooperate. Yet the claim prevails that, at some moment long ago, mindless minerals somehow overcame the basic laws of chemistry and probability, and formed a suitable primordial soup that enabled the purely naturalistic synthesis of a living cell. We should apply the tests of truth or fiction to such a claim.

The First Cell

Let us assume that the hypothetical primordial soup formed, and all the necessary left-handed proteins and other molecular raw ingredients for a living cell also spontaneously formed, folded themselves correctly, and gathered together into one place for a brief period of time.

The next part of the evolutionary story is that these ingredients then structured themselves, purely through random motion, into the phenomenally complex component assemblies that made up the functioning nanotechnology of the first living cell, and life began. We need to appreciate a simple reality. Chemicals outside living cells will denature without the protection afforded by the cell. They will 'roll down the hill' into lower states of equilibrium. So, the arrival of the first living cell with the information and nanomachinery that enable it to be self-sustaining (and self-replicating) is the starting point of life.

When Darwin published his theory of evolution, the understanding of a basic cell was that it was a simple blob of protoplasm. Today we are starting to appreciate the sheer scale of complexity in a cell – which is comparable to the infrastructures of a small city – and the astonishingly sophisticated nanotechnology that is essential for even the simplest bacterium. This nanotechnology requires three-dimensional organised structure, which is not a natural property of the component protein molecules. If left to themselves in a sterile solution, proteins do not organise themselves into the machinery of life of their own accord. No one has yet demonstrated how a cell membrane could form spontaneously, with all the necessary pumps and other nanomachinery to maintain a chemical composition inside that is different from the external environment.[8] In addition, a myriad of other components are essential for a viable self-replicating cell, and these would also need to form inside that first cell membrane.

Within living cells today, all the various components were originally manufactured, assembled, and organised by the amazing nanomachinery of its parent. They were then maintained by the new cell's own nanomachinery. The first living cell, of course, had

---

8. It is actually far more complicated than this. The cell membranes of bacteria and archaea also need special mechanisms to generate an electric charge. This in turn drives millions of ATP synthase motors that must be attached to their inner wall so that these can manufacture the necessary ATP molecules to power all the other cellular machinery.

no such parent. We can't sensibly appeal to random motion to be the parent, because of three inconvenient realities:

- Random motion destroys structure. Over time, things will degenerate into a purely random equilibrium. Contrary to the commonly heard evolutionary claim,[9] 'enough time' will not allow the impossible to occur in a chemical solution. Instead, enough time will ensure that even something quite simple will *never* happen in a solution that has attained equilibrium.
- There is no incremental path to the first living cell. It has been well documented that the second law of thermodynamics also applies to biomolecular solutions. So, until the assembly of the first cell attained the threshold where it became self-sustaining through its own nanomachinery, using energy obtained from the local environment or the sun, the entire process would roll back down the hill.
- The probability of sufficient structure to kick-start a living bacterium being assembled through purely random motion is incalculably small. Amino acids must be polymerised in the correct sequence in order to form billions of useful proteins, which must all be folded correctly. These proteins must then be assembled into thousands of identical copies of various nanomachines, which in turn must be located correctly within the overall structure of the cell. Even if we were talking vastly optimistic improbabilities in the order

---

9. 'Time is the hero of the plot ... Given so much time, the impossible becomes possible, the possible becomes probable, the probable becomes virtually certain. One only has to wait; time itself performs miracles.' Wald, G. (1954, August). The origin of life. *Scientific American*, p. 45.

of 1 in 10 followed by a trillion zeros, say, this would still equate to winning a lottery from all the electrons in the universe more than ten billion times *in a row*.

The basic laws of chemistry create further fundamental problems. A solution of *nucleotides*[10] has no propensity to assemble itself randomly into double-helix structures.[11] This structure is achieved in a cell only by very complex nanomachinery that is still not fully understood, which merely makes a copy of the existing double-helix during cell-division. Furthermore, the hypothetical primordial soup would not be a pure solution of nucleotides. Many of the other necessary molecules present in the soup would react adversely with nucleotides. Nevertheless, nucleotides would have somehow needed to assemble themselves into a double-helix structure (which also represented meaningful information!) as yet another essential component during the formation of the hypothetical first cell.

ATP creates another huge chicken-and-egg problem. All cellular machinery is powered by ATP. Yet ATP cannot form naturally. It requires the remarkable *ATP synthase* enzyme[12] to manufacture it.

---

10. Nucleotides are the molecules that form the building blocks of DNA – adenine, cytosine, guanine and thymine – and are represented by the letters A, C, G and T in sequenced genetic code. Three nucleotides group together to form a *codon* which identifies the amino acid that should appear at a certain point in the protein molecule specified by that portion of the DNA.
11. A full double-helix structure of DNA would be essential in a hypothetical first cell. Otherwise it would have no mechanism to reliably reproduce itself during the first cell division or to reproduce in subsequent generations.
12. This enzyme is a rotary nanomotor. If you are not familiar with it, Google 'ATP synthase'. A number of sites have animations that help visualise how it works, and understand the problems for its spontaneous construction in a prebiotic soup.

The first cell could not even begin to start working until there was a sufficient concentration of ATP in its cytoplasm. However, ATP synthase needs raw materials to work on, especially ADP. ADP is synthesised in a complex 10-step process called *glycolysis*, which requires several other special enzymes. Significantly, steps one and three in this process require energy from ATP. How then could our hypothetical first cell pull its energy level up by the bootstraps from an initial zero state to the minimum concentration for cellular viability? We don't yet understand how new ATP synthase nanomachines are assembled in a living cell. Even the most primitive hypothetical first cell would need millions of them to be viable. How could even one ATP synthase machine have been assembled by the random sloshing of our hypothetical primordial soup? But these ATP synthase motors won't even work if they are just floating around in the cytoplasm. They must be fixed to a membrane[13] that has an electric charge across it, which powers their 'motor'. Evolutionists have yet to demonstrate a valid mechanism that would enable random processes to create such an electric charge during the assembly of the hypothetical first cell.

Bacteria today have the ability to synthesise some amino acids. To be viable and grow, the first cell would also need to synthesise all the amino acids that it could not scavenge in sufficient quantity from the primordial soup. This further increases the degree of difficulty. However, it is difficult to conceive how random molecular motion could assemble the mechanism to synthesise even one amino acid. Given no biosphere existed at that time, which could take a 'team approach' to this problem as today, the first cell would

13. In bacteria they are attached to the inside wall of the cell's external membrane. In higher life forms (plants and animals) they are attached to the outside of mitochondria which generate the necessary electric gradient.

be on its own. Being realistic, random motion would somehow need to give the first cell mechanisms to synthesise at least ten of the more difficult amino acids. Of course, this still presupposes that all twenty amino acids were present in sufficient quantities to build the protein molecules that needed them when the first cell was spontaneously assembled and kick-started into life. These are huge assumptions that have not been validated by experimental science.

Nitrogen is an essential element in all amino acids. However, molecular nitrogen is very stable. In the current biosphere, specialised microorganisms perform one of the most remarkable reactions in biochemistry, breaking down molecular nitrogen into a form that is useful to the rest of the biosphere. If the first cell needed to manufacture any amino acids, it would have needed to solve the nitrogen problem as well. Even if we assume that the hypothetical first cell did not need to manufacture any amino acids, it is difficult to imagine how the chemistry of life could continue to depend on external sources for the rare amino acids in subsequent generations. The need to devise its own mechanism to solve the nitrogen problem in order to replicate and thrive would create another huge degree of difficulty for our hypothetical first cell. Furthermore, if such an essential, valuable capability was established in the earliest of life forms, why has it not been retained by the majority of life forms rather than the whole biosphere becoming dependent on a few crucial bacteria? The loss of vital capabilities that improve survival fitness goes against the basic tenets of evolution. Does this suggest the whole first-cell hypothesis is flawed, because life requires a team approach where multiple life forms need to work together to overcome fundamental problems?

There is yet another significant hurdle for our hypothetical first cell. It is not enough for it to merely be viable through having the ability to sustain itself by using nutrients and energy from its external environment. It would also need the highly complex physical mechanisms and matching control systems that would enable it to survive completely haemorrhaging itself in two, in the process of cell division. Otherwise it would be an irrelevant dead end. The entire process of cell division would need to work correctly on the first attempt; there is no margin for error. As a professional software developer, I would view with utter incredulity any claim that a mission-critical control system of that complexity could be delivered without any testing and remedial fixes whatsoever – even by the highest calibre software team on the planet. Yet we are asked to accept that mindless chemicals were able to achieve this through purely random activity. Alternatively, how many spontaneous viable cells would have come and gone as irrelevant dead ends, before one of them somehow accidentally pulled off the first successful cell division? Then how many of those would need to come and go before the vital keys were accidentally preserved in the DNA and nanomachinery, so that subsequent generations could both replicate and pass on this ability? Successful cell division poses a huge *extra* degree of difficulty for the hypothetical random processes. What are our conclusions when we apply tests of truth or fiction to this aspect of the evolution story?

Modern scientific observation has taught us much about fundamental chemistry. Do we observe organic molecules experimenting in a manner necessary to spontaneously assemble themselves into the first living, reproducing cell? No! They follow laws. We can be very glad that molecules do not behave out of character. Otherwise, they would lose the stability on which organic life depends, and we would not have made it past the first few seconds in our mother's womb.

Do scientific observations of the real world support atheistic claims that the very first living cell could arise spontaneously in a primordial soup, or do they tend to expose them as highly suspect? Instead, do scientific observations actually provide signposts that point to the conclusion that life was created by someone outside the system? It is appropriate to use the word 'someone' rather than something, because life's creative source would obviously need to have extraordinary intelligence and nanoengineering ability.[14]

---

14. This is a big subject. It can easily be explored more deeply via the Internet. Search for *chemical evolution*, *origin of life*, *abiogenesis* and *abiogenesis problems* to get both sides of the debate. However, whenever you encounter terminology like *perhaps*, *might*, *may have* or *could have*, it indicates what you are reading is storytelling rather than observational science. Yet this is more honest than the presumption that presents partially-informed guesswork as infallible scientific facts, such as 'Three billion years ago, such and such happened…' It is difficult to discern motives but always wise to test for truth – does this writer approach the subject with humility and integrity that is eager to recalibrate himself or herself according to what he or she discovers, or is he or she on a mission to protect some rigid, non-negotiable starting assumptions?

Life and Biosphere:

Organisms

The First Organism

An organism is a vastly more complex system than a single bacterium because its cells are differentiated. For example, muscle cells differ from those in the neural network which, in turn, are very different again from those in digestive membranes. The cells are structurally arranged according to a functional body plan. Cells that are deep within the organism cannot obtain essential nutrients directly from the environment. So an organism, whether plant or animal, needs integrated systems to extract nutrients from the external environment, deliver them to every one of its cells, and remove and excrete waste products. This is the rudimentary starting point for any organism. What then would drive the development towards the *first* organism? A colony of bacteria would have far greater survival and reproductive fitness than any of the conceivable half-way houses on a hypothetical evolutionary pathway to the first organism. Natural selection would work against an experiment that required many generations before success was achieved.

The first organism would also have needed very sophisticated control mechanisms for both its initial reproduction and the coordinated development of its progeny from their embryonic stages. If the first hypothetical organism was capable of controlled movement, or other physical response to the environment, then it would need a functional neural system to achieve this – even one as primitive as that found in a jellyfish, which has no central brain. The first organism would also need to survive the seasonal and other climatic variations in its natural environment, even in the ocean. This would have required additional capabilities and control systems that gave the necessary flexibility to survive in the real world. Because the plant and animal kingdoms are so different, in almost every aspect, it would seem that bacteria would have needed to pull off this huge step-up to an organism twice!

The foundational physical structures, control systems, and supporting extra information in the DNA that define a functional organism, are a huge step-up from a colony of simple bacteria. How credible are evolutionary claims that sporadic mutations are a plausible mechanism for incrementally adding vast amounts of highly matched new information to the DNA that supports control systems for cell differentiation, multiple and mutually essential metabolic systems, coordinated growth according to a body plan, and passing on the new advances to the next generation? How credible is the secondary claim that this process could be advanced via a long continuous sequence of viable, self-replicating, intermediate life forms – which were *all* favoured by natural selection?

If we reflect on the nature of a system, we find it has multiple matching components that must all be present, and functioning optimally, for the system to work. If any of the essential components are missing, the whole system is not viable. For example, the absence of a single comma will cause a computer program to crash, whether it has thousands of lines of source code or only ten. Systems must be tuned as an integrated whole, in order to work well – or even to work at all. We often overlook this, because we don't see the design effort that went into products that we buy, but we are reminded of this reality when our car is hard to start. Finally, a system is vulnerable to its weakest component, from a single break in a light bulb filament to the failure of an O-ring or tile on a space shuttle. This understanding about systems should be applied to claims that once-upon-a-time bacteria somehow evolved into a system, especially a system with the complexity of a basic organism.

Modern science has given us much knowledge about bacteria. So, do we observe them continually experimenting in a manner and at a rate required to transform themselves into an organism? Could bacteria really develop incrementally into an organism as the essential next stage in Darwin's *tree of life*? Do our scientific observations of the real world support evolutionary claims in this regard, or do our observations show them up as highly suspect? Is scientific documentation of the gulf between bacteria and higher life forms a signpost that points to a creator?

Sexual Reproduction

Sexual reproduction is common throughout the biosphere. It facilitates diversity within a population, increasing its adaptability to changes in the environment and its ability to move into other habitats. Yet there are several curly questions:

- What would drive the transition from the efficient, asexual reproductive mechanism of bacteria and some simple organisms to the new specialised sexual mechanism?
- Sexual reproduction requires highly specialised and compatible male and female sexual apparatus, and the process is vastly different from asexual reproduction. How could this transition between the two very different processes develop incrementally?
- The mechanisms for sexual reproduction across the different kingdoms of the biosphere are very different. Flowering and

fruiting plants are particularly problematic, because their mechanisms are doubly dependent on both the insect and animal kingdoms, and further complicated by the need to target either birds or mammals to distribute the seeds. This suggests that the transition from asexual reproduction must have occurred independently several times if it is to be explained within the evolutionary paradigm. Yet it is difficult to envisage the transition occurring even once through natural processes, let alone several times.

- Sexual reproduction has an advantage only when there is an existing population with significantly more genetic information/diversity in its gene pool than possessed by any one individual (unlike a colony of bacteria which are usually genetically identical). How could significant genetic diversity arise within a local asexual population? It is debatable whether beneficial mutations actually exist which could take populations 'uphill' by either reproductive mechanism.[1] Even if they do exist, it is then debatable whether uphill mutations could have created and established sufficient diversity quickly enough. So, there is a chicken-or-egg problem: nothing existed to drive the transition to sexual reproduction until a new mechanism, such as sexual reproduction itself, helped to produce genetic diversity within the population. More importantly, how could sexual reproduction be established simultaneously across a significant segment of an asexual population, such that it could then capitalise on any diversity within it and provide a survival advantage?

---

1. This will be discussed in depth later, as a separate section – see 'Mutations'.

- Since we observe sexual reproduction in all the kingdoms of the biosphere except that of bacteria, does it support the evolution story, or is it another signpost that points to genuine design?

Life and Biosphere:

Bio Information

We live in a very exciting period of human history. The ability to sequence genomes of humans, animals, plants and bacteria has opened many new frontiers in medical and scientific research. It has also revealed many things that are very inconvenient for the story of evolution.

For example, the chimpanzee genome is actually 12 percent larger than ours, which challenges the truthfulness of the frequent claim that there is less than one percent difference between the two genomes. Further, the Y chromosomes are approximately 53 percent different in their gene counts – humans have 78 genes and chimps only 37![1] Evolutionary assumptions demand that the Y chromosome must be extremely unstable for such a huge change to occur within the five to eight million years since human and chimpanzee lines are thought to have separated. This resulted in the rotting Y chromosome hypothesis. However, recent research has shown that Y chromosomes are actually very stable, and that hypothesis has been debunked. The demonstrated stability of the Y chromosome, together with the huge difference between the genomes, poses a significant challenge to the evolutionary story about our human ancestry.

---

1. Hughes, J. F. (2010). Chimpanzee and human Y chromosomes are remarkably divergent in structure and gene content." *Nature*, 463, 536–9. doi: 10.1038/nature08700.

The human genome has approximately three billion base pairs or letters. Three billion letters is a huge amount of information.[2] The genomes of bacteria are understandably much smaller, ranging between 140,000 and 14 million letters and averaging about four million letters. Bacteria with less than 600,000 letters are dependent on other bacteria to build various essential biomolecules, and therefore are not candidates for a viable, self-replicating first cell. Even 600,000 letters is a lot of information.[3] How could this information arise all by itself as an integrated and essential part of the nanotechnology of the hypothetical first cell?

Information is independent of the medium on which it is stored. Sequences of the representative letters in DNA can also be stored on a computer hard drive, displayed on a screen, and portions transmitted by email and read aloud by human voice (definitely very small portions). Information is not in any way defined by the medium on which it is stored. The recipient of the information needs to 'understand' what the coding scheme represents. In digital information technology, binary ones and zeros form the base for standard computer codes such as ASCII, EBCDIC, and Unicode. These codes are quite different from one another. For example, the binary equivalent of the decimal number 75 represents a capital *K* in ASCII but a full stop in EBCDIC. The number 122 represents a lower-case *z* in ASCII but a colon in EBCDIC. Programs written to work with ASCII input files cannot understand EBCDIC files, and vice versa. Computers work correctly when the coding system matches the software, and crash when it doesn't.

---

2. Three gigabytes equates to approximately 10,000 average-sized paperbacks. But if stored as pure binary code, one byte could store four letters of genetic code, and the human genome would then occupy 750 megabytes.
3. 600,000 letters is nearly double the size of this book.

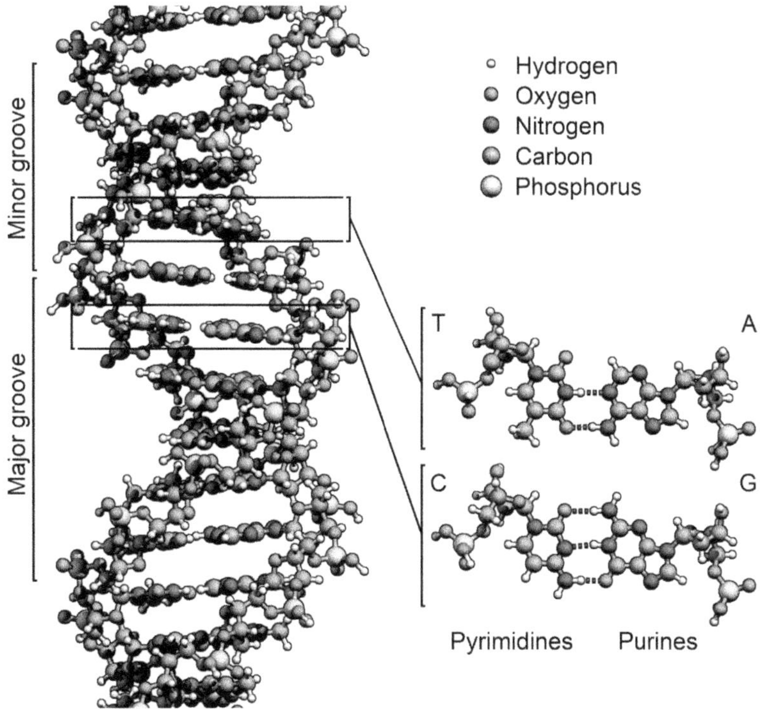

Figure 4. Graphic representation of a short length of DNA.

Similarly, the letters in DNA don't mean anything on their own. They merely provide the base mechanism for genetic code, in much the same way that binary numbers provide the base mechanisms for different computer coding systems. Living cells have two highly complex and specialised machines (RNA polymerase and ribosomes) that work *in tandem* to transcribe sections of the genetic code into the amino acid sequences (proteins) that they specify. However, cells don't just have one of each machine. To produce copious quantities of their thousand or so different but essential proteins at the rate necessary for cellular viability, living cells (including bacteria) have tens of thousands of identical copies of these machines, working simultaneously on different parts of the genome.

No one has ever scientifically demonstrated that information can arise from randomly jumbling component letters together. In the world of signals and communications, random changes are called *noise*. Noise always corrupts and *destroys* existing information; it never creates completely new information. The end result of random activity over time is *random equilibrium*. In the context of information, random equilibrium means complete *garbage*.

Information is all about meaning and purpose. Obviously, it is not a property of any of the raw materials of this universe – protons, electrons, atoms, molecules, photons, or energy. Random processes destroy rather than create information. Yet information is an essential distinctive of life. So, how could the vast volume of information in the biosphere come into existence? Is bioinformation a large signpost that points to an author of that information?

Genetic Information for the First Cell

If there was no author, the first cell in the evolution story would have needed to randomly assemble more than 600,000 letters[4] of extremely well-structured, relevant, and meaningful information.

---

4. In a software context, 600,000 letters equate to about 25,000 lines of computer source code. For 'normal' computer software, this would take somewhere from three to ten man-years to write. However, the software of life provides instructions to machines that assemble long complex molecules and fold them correctly in three-dimensions, exposing just the right lengths in just the right places, so they can perform chemical magic as enzymes. This is in a completely different league of difficulty. One might ask how many humans would possess the intellectual capacity to write a full genome of such software: it would be zero. (Perhaps random processes have as much chance as we would, after all.☺)

While there are a number of bacteria with small genomes of this length, the number of viable genomes is miniscule when compared to the vast number of other random permutations. Assuming that almost every letter would have been relevant – the idea that most DNA is junk was shown up as a serious mistake about a decade ago[5] – then the probability of a functional genome for the first cell having formed through purely random activity is approximately one in ten followed by more than 350,000 zeros.[6] This would equate to winning our cosmic electron lottery about 4,500 times *in a row*, or a national mega lottery 45,000 weeks in a row buying a single ticket each week.[7] However, without an almost perfect genome stored in its DNA, our first hypothetical cell would not have been viable. Furthermore, its genome must also have been assembled in virtually the same instant that the thousands of identical ribosomes and other matching cell machines were somehow also formed by random motion. This would also need to be the same instant that they were completely enclosed, together with millions of enzymes, by a randomly created cell membrane that prevented this biotech treasure from being lost through dispersion into the wider soup.

The Coding Scheme

This subsection is provided primarily for readers who, like me, have a software engineering bent. While it has been written in a manner that should be understandable and interesting for other readers, feel free to speed-read through it, or skip over it completely.

---

5. This is a noteworthy example of how evolutionary thinking has often created filters that hindered the progress of science.
6. The probability that 600,000 random DNA letters specify a working genome is approximately 1 in $4^{600,000} = 10^{350,000}$
7. This is simple compared with the improbability of assembling all the cell machinery through random motion.

The original cell would first need to establish its own coding scheme to store its information. It would then somehow also need to create all the necessary information using this scheme exclusively.

There are a vast number of possible binary coding schemes that could be used with computers. However, thanks to collaborative work by major players in the computer industry, only three primary ones are now used: ASCII, Unicode, and EBCDIC. This standardisation involved significant design effort by highly intelligent engineers. Purely random processes are not capable of such a venture.

In the same way, there are a vast number of possible coding schemes for the codons – triplets of letters – that code to amino acids. There are quintillions of possible entry-level coding systems alone. However, the coding scheme that is used by all life has built-in redundancy, where every one of the 64 permutations code back to one of the 20 amino acids. The number of possible coding systems like this is in the order of 10^{90} – that is 1 followed by 90 zeros, or ten billion times the number of electrons in the known universe. Are you starting to get a sense of the degree of improbability for random activity to assemble all the nucleotides of the entire genome of the first cell in a way that represented meaningful information when understood exclusively using a single DNA coding system?

But, even more significantly, every one of the original ribosomes supposedly assembled by random processes would need to perfectly, and exclusively, match the coding system of the original DNA. There is no reason why each randomly assembled ribosome – if such a thing was possible – would not instead have come together in a way that worked with a completely different coding system. If just five percent of the ribosomes were 'singing to different tunes', this would probably be lethal for any hypothetical first cell. Living cells need lots of ribosomes in order to manufacture their considerable variety of essential proteins at the rate necessary for viability. Mammals can have up to 10 million ribosomes in each cell.

Bacteria like E. coli typically have between ten thousand and seventy thousand, depending on how rapidly they are growing. The smallest bacteria have approximately one thousand ribosomes. This would seem to be the bottom limit of viability, and therefore the 'level of the bar' for the hypothetical first cell. The discussion in the next few paragraphs is predicated on this assumption, which is difficult to either verify or invalidate.

When a new cell emerges from the process of cell division, all its original ribosomes come from its parent. However, within its DNA and existing cell machinery, it possesses all it needs to build new ribosomes. The primordial soup hypothesis requires some other mechanism to build enough identically functioning ribosomes for the first cell to be viable. Any halfway-house precursors to a cell, that could reproduce ribosomes from templates, are ruled out because they would require all the supporting infrastructures of an entire fully functional cell. Biomolecules don't naturally arrange themselves into molecular machinery. As mentioned earlier, random motion destroys structure. Yet the only purely naturalistic mechanism remaining, for the origin of the first cell's ribosomes and other nanomachinery, is random molecular motion.

The improbability of just 1,000 randomly assembled ribosomes all happening to use the same single genetic coding scheme as the randomly assembled DNA genome, out of so many possible schemes, is vast. It is about 1 in 1 followed by 90,000 zeros ($10^{90,000}$), which equates to winning our electron in the universe lottery more than 1,100 times *in a row*. Of course, the improbability of random molecular motion assembling millions of organic molecules into 1,000 identically functioning ribosomes is light years beyond this again.

In reality, some of those coding systems would be impossible to implement in a workable ribosome, although the random mechanisms that supposedly chose the coding system for the DNA would not 'know' which ones were practical. However, no researcher has ever demonstrated how even one functioning ribosome could be assembled through purely random particle motion within a sterilised mixture of the necessary proteins, RNA, and sugars. Given the observed behaviour of molecules within such a mixture, we can reasonably expect that no one will ever do so.

Interestingly, the coding scheme of life[8] has been shown to be the best possible for redundancy and error avoidance. Many single letter-copying errors will result in the original amino acid still being used, or one with similar characteristics that will work almost as well. Supposedly this optimal coding system was chosen completely by chance out of 10^{90} possible schemes, because it would be implausible for the coding scheme common to all life to have subsequently been tweaked by natural processes. A single change of understanding in the transcription machinery of a bacterium would be disastrous unless it was simultaneously matched by more than 10,000 identical substitution mutations of all related codons across the entire genome. However, a bacterial cell has approximately 20,000 ribosomes – constituting about a quarter of its mass – because living cells need to do a lot of parallel processing to simultaneously produce numerous copies of many different proteins. Even if our first cells still had only the minimum 1,000 ribosomes to be viable, how would such a change of understanding be achieved simultaneously across all of those ribosomes?[9]

Consider the optimal nature of the common coding convention, and its exclusive use throughout the entire hypothetical first genome. Consider also the need for every part of the first cell's inde-

---

8. 'CAT' represents histidine, 'GGT' glycine, 'GTG' valine, etc.
9. There are actually a few organisms that use variations of the common code. However, no-one has demonstrated how these different coding systems could have viably developed within the evolutionary paradigm – and in this too are unlikely to ever do so, for the reasons just given.

pendently assembled transcription and protein-folding machinery to match it perfectly – and not just once, since many identically functioning copies of the machinery are necessary for viability from the outset. Finally, reflect on the nature of the information itself: specifying wonder working enzymes that only function when folded correctly in three dimensions, and much more. All these factors combine to create a galactic degree of difficulty for chance and purely random molecular motion to overcome. Is this another signpost that points to genuine design and exquisitely detailed nanoconstruction by a colossally intelligent software engineer?

Views from this Vantage Point

While we are here in our travel guide, it is probably worth contemplating the nuts and bolts of the origin of life a little further. RNA polymerase and ribosomes are only part of the cellular orchestra. As mentioned in the section on the primordial soup, when protein strands emerge from the ribosome, further nanotechnology takes over to complete protein manufacture. A whole suite of different chaperone molecules prevent the proteins from folding prematurely and incorrectly. Then cellular machines called chaperonins fold them correctly in three dimensions so that they can serve their purpose. If you are not familiar with the basic workings of a cell I recommend that you spend a whole evening here in your road map to explore this.[10] What has been discovered over the last few decades is truly mind-boggling.

---

10. Google these three cellular machine names: *RNA polymerase*, *ribosome*, and *chaperonin*. Try Wikipedia or www.nigms.nih.gov/education/cells/. Then search again adding the keyword *image* or *animation*. Be aware that most animations are greatly simplified compared with the real thing. Other cellular machines worth investigating are *ATP synthase* and *kinesin motor protein*.

Once you have a basic feel for the complexity of the cellular machines, try to envisage one of these marvels of nanotechnology being thrown together in just the right way as a consequence of purely random molecular motion and microscopic eddy currents within the sloshing of a hypothetical primordial soup.[11] Then try to envisage *thousands* of *identical* copies of each of the above five machines simultaneously appearing in very close proximity by the same purely random mechanisms. These identical machines all need to match their common template at least in function. They must match exactly with the protein coding and other information contained within the DNA. This in turn must also contain the information necessary to make additional copies of these nanomachines. Numerous enzymes must also be present to facilitate the basic chemistry essential in the construction and function of these machines. Many additional types of cellular machines are also essential in any viable cell – and nearly a billion ATP synthase machines would be required. Finally, try to envisage a functional, external cell membrane forming immediately to completely contain the new machines and enzymes before they rapidly dispersed due to the random motion of particles in a large solution. Together these form just a few foundational requirements that are simplistically taken for granted as axiomatic assumptions in the naturalistic story of the origin of life. Is this sensible, or does it beggar belief?

The difficulties for a naturalistic origin of protein and DNA-based life are so great that many scientists currently favour the *RNA world hypothesis*. This postulates an initial, simpler halfway house (or 'billionth-way' house, if you prefer) based merely on RNA, rather than proteins and DNA. It goes on to claim that *life*

---

11. This would require the primordial soup to be comprised of nicely folded full-length and exclusively left-handed proteins, rather than a racemic mixture of free amino acids and short chains of them.

– now redefined as merely self-replicating molecules rather than cells – subsequently progressed from there to the DNA world that we observe today. Several discoveries fit with this hypothesis,[12] and have been used to argue in its favour. Others are seriously problematic for it. For example, protein enzymes are needed to overcome several significant hurdles in basic chemistry during the synthesis of RNA in living cells. And the RNA world is still affected by the same foundational problem as the DNA world: how could random processes create information and write software? In a delightful play on Winston Churchill's famous quote about democracy, it has been said that, 'The RNA world hypothesis is the worst theory of the early evolution of life, except for all the others.'[13] The RNA world hypothesis is another side-excursion that you may like to come back to and explore later. If you do, bear in mind that, when applying tests for truth or fiction, we should be wary of schools of thought that need to redefine commonly understood terminology to mean something more convenient for their purposes. It is usually a warning sign of errant thinking, even deception. Our threshold for something that can appropriately be called life should be a self-replicating system that has information and nanomachinery along with the necessary enzymes that enable all its basic chemistry to work. The onus is on the claimants to demonstrate that RNA-based

---

12. In the early 1980s research groups led by Sidney Altman and Thomas Cech independently found that RNAs can also act as catalysts for some chemical reactions. More recently it was discovered that, while ribosomes contain both RNA and proteins, the peptide bonds it uses to build protein chains are catalysed by RNA, not proteins. Retrieved from exploringorigins.org/ribozymes.html.
13. Bernhardt, HS (2012). The RNA world hypothesis is the worst theory of the early evolution of life (except for all the others). Biology Direct, 7 (23). doi: 10.1186/1745-6150-7-23 www.ncbi.nlm.nih.gov/pmc/articles/PMC3495036/.

chemistry has the capability to produce a viable *system* with these attributes.

For all the hypothesising that RNA might have formed some self-replicating chemicals as the precursors to life, it would seem that the starting point for *genuine* life still has to be a viable cell. Without information and nanomachinery to enable the first cell to be self-sustaining, all the hypothetical chemical achievements would have rolled back down the hill into a state of equilibrium that conformed to the chemical behaviours observed today. As already discussed, the spontaneous starting point for life would also have needed to possess the colossally complex control systems necessary for successful cell division. Anything less than this would have been a dead-end, a wondrous fizzer.

The threshold for the spontaneous origin of a living cell on Earth was so high, even back in the 1960s and 70s, that a number of leading scientists at that time abandoned this hypothesis in favour of *panspermia.*[14] These scientists included Francis Crick, the co-discoverer of DNA's structure, and the astronomer Sir Fred Hoyle. But naturalistic panspermia has huge additional problems, such as the extreme improbability of a direct hit on Earth from a star system even 100 light years away. The probability of something randomly ejected from our own sun hitting the earth is only one in 2.4 billion. Hitting Earth from 100 light years away is more than forty trillion times less likely again. The probability of doing so is about the same as winning a mega lottery three weeks in a row with

14. Panspermia is the belief that life began in a more favourable planet in our galaxy, and somehow made its way to earth inside a meteor, or a capsule sent by an advanced extra-terrestrial civilization. (The proponents of directed panspermia tacitly acknowledge that a highly intelligent external agent was essential in the origin of life – they just attribute it to ET.)

a single ticket each time. An interstellar cell would also need to survive the billion-year journey in a frigid vacuum, and its fiery arrival on Earth. The ET version has more going for it in this regard!

In addition, there are plausibility issues with panspermia's foundational assumptions:

- that a more favourable planet for life than Earth exists somewhere else in the universe (more than that, somewhere very close by in our own galaxy);
- that the 'show-stoppers' for an Earth-bound origin of life would not be applicable on another planet; and
- that the diverse biosphere we observe around us could actually have developed from a single seed of life.

One wonders what a more favourable planet would actually look like, given the exquisite suitability of Earth for life. Further, another planet would still be subject to the same laws of chemistry, physics, statistical mathematics, and information as our own.

While the spontaneous origin of life on Earth was already too high a bar for a number of top scientists back in the 1960s, the explosion of discovery about the chemistry and nanotechnology of life in the half-century since then has raised the bar by many orders of magnitude.

Information is an essential component and characteristic of all life, as is its extremely tight integration with the cell machinery. Yet information clearly cannot arise from random activity of atoms and molecules – even on a hypothetically 'more conducive' planet for the origin of life. So, does the sheer volume and specialised nature of the information essential in the first cell support the evolution story? Or is it another signpost pointing to an author of that information as well as genuine design by a *very* intelligent and competent creator?

If life on Earth was created in situ by an intelligent agent, then there is no need for all life forms to have developed from a single first cell. Various life forms could have been created simultaneously with common design principles and features, just as independent car manufacturers have concluded that four wheels is the optimum design for most small vehicles. Evolutionists see commonalities such as eyes and four legs as evidence of common descent. Is it possible that they are, instead, evidence of common design?

However, let's stick with the evolution paradigm for now. If, against all odds, a viable, self-replicating first cell assembled itself in a primordial soup, or arrived inside a meteor, is it reasonable to believe that purely naturalistic processes could then have progressively developed this into all the life forms, and functioning biosphere, that we now observe? This thesis will be explored in the next few sections.

Genetic Information and New Species

The volume of genetic information in the biosphere across all kingdoms, genera, and species is colossal. Sure, commonalities exist – even between humans and bananas. After factoring out overlaps, the amount of unique genetic information across the estimated 50 million species in the current biosphere is still vast. If we include all the extinct species in the fossil record, the total volume of unique information spanning biological history is significantly greater again. Even allowing for lots of parallel development, do the currently hypothesised mechanisms have any chance of producing this volume of information within even the oldest estimate for the age of the Earth?

In this section of the road map we will look at mutations, speciation, and natural selection from a genetic information perspective. We will assess the plausibility of the oft-repeated claim that mutations combine with natural selection to produce vast amounts of new genetic information which, over time, accumulate into new bio-kingdoms, families, and species.

Mutations

According to the reigning evolutionary paradigm,[15] mutations are the source of new information added into Darwin's tree of life. Natural selection then favoured the beneficial mutations, which accumulated over time into new innovations such as roots, stems, leaves, flowers, limbs, eyes, ears, fur, wings, and every other novelty we observe in the natural world. But does our current scientific and medical knowledge of mutations and their effects support this paradigm?

Most mutations are random changes via deletions, substitutions, and sometimes insertions of a single DNA base pair in either the genome or mitochondria. In some cases they can be a duplication of a lengthy sequence of DNA. As previously mentioned, random changes to information equate to noise, and they destroy original information. Most mutations are harmful: they cause miscarriage, death or severe disability immediately in the mutant offspring, or cause harm farther down the track when recessive genes ultimately find expression. Most evolutionists readily acknowledge this. It is what we would reasonably expect if random changes were made to the 'software of life', just as if random changes were made to computer software. It is also what we observe in reality; medical and scientific literature documents hundreds of thousands of mutations. These have all been classified as either harmful, or having no observed effect on function. This is very inconvenient for the

15. This is usually called *Modern Synthesis* in scientific circles. Essentially it is the Neo-Darwinism of the late 1800s and early 1900s with a few minor tweaks.

evolution story, since not even one has yet been identified that has provided an improvement to function in the wild.

Claims are often made that some mutations, such as superbugs that cause problems in hospitals, are evidence of uphill evolution. However, these mutants have damaged metabolisms which do not absorb standard antibiotics. Being much weaker, they would not survive in normal environments where they faced competition from other bacteria or attack from healthy human immune systems. (These mutations should not be confused with the other form of antibiotic resistance, which is merely due to natural selection rather than mutations. Poor use of antibiotics allows already existing resistant strains to survive and reproduce. These also are colloquially called superbugs.) Bacteria digesting the waste products from Nylon manufacture are often touted as examples of mutations creating a new function. However, the claim is doubtful. It is likely these bacteria already possessed a pre-programmed ability to adapt to new environments.[16]

Assuming beneficial mutations are still theoretically possible, the ratio of harmful mutations to good ones creates a huge statistical problem. For instance, if the ratio was 100,000 harmful mutations for every beneficial one,[17] then the improbability of a new innovation that required only 1,000 beneficial mutations making it out the far end would be 1 in $10^{5,000}$ (i.e. 1 followed by 5,000 zeros). However, most biological innovations would require far more than 1,000 new nucleotides of information to be added to the

---

16. See creation.com/the-adaptation-of-bacteria-to-feeding-on-nylon-waste for a good summary of the more significant problems, and why existing built-in flexibility is a more likely explanation.
17. One good mutation in 100,000 is probably being very generous to evolutionists. Current documentation of known mutations suggests that 1 in 500,000 might be more realistic.

genome before any beneficial new functionality could be achieved. Evolutionists appeal to natural selection at this point, claiming that it would have progressively culled any harmful mutations that arose and favoured the beneficial ones. This idea seems slightly plausible at first glance. But it would be very difficult for a favourable individual mutation to become fixed in a population, so it could be built on by subsequent generations. Even if this did occur, the success rate would fall short of what would be necessary to accumulate the biosphere's current volume of genetic information within a maximum time frame of even four billion years.

This problem was first identified by JBS Haldane in 1957, when he attempted to calculate limits for the speed of beneficial evolution, and became known as *Haldane's dilemma*. Many websites which support creation and intelligent design use this as an argument against evolution. However, research published since 1957 has identified factors that Haldane had overlooked. Further, several computer models have been developed, where the parameters can be tweaked in a way that makes everything fit within four billion years. The issue cannot yet be resolved definitively, because these calculations are all purely theoretical, and there is enough 'wiggle' room to make them produce whatever results one wants. We are talking about unobserved hypothetical changes that supposedly occurred over aeons of time and, up until now, it has not been possible to conduct scientific experiments that furnish the actual values that should be used for respective parameters in those computer models. Perhaps over the next decade or so, studies using genome sequencing may help bring some clarity to this corner of the debate. The foundational claim that mutations can create a vast amount of new and meaningful information desperately needs verification. If this claim is false, then computer models attempting to calculate how long it might take to accumulate the necessary information through mutations would obviously be modelling a fantasy.

The quantity of extra information required for new, functional innovations should not be underestimated. New limbs, senses, and other innovations require extensive networks of new genes, and the addition of intricate new control systems to re-engineer seed or embryonic development. In the animal kingdom, new neural pathways and a new processing region in the brain would also be essential for real functionality. According to the theory of evolution, this information accumulates a few mutations per generation over many generations. However, each incremental step (mutation) must create a significant survival advantage such that it would be favoured, rather than eliminated, by natural selection. Also, each new 'advance' must be significant so that it quickly becomes fixed into that local population, and subsequent generations can then build on it. The need for multiple new networks of genes creates a fundamental problem. Until the right combination of multiple mutations occurred, there would be no resulting benefit for natural selection to favour. Furthermore, promising lines must also survive the likelihood of being killed off downstream by lethal or dysfunctional mutations, given that the overwhelming majority of mutations are harmful rather than benign.

Recessive mutations create an even more serious problem, simply because the majority of mutations are recessive. While natural selection cannot favour any beneficial mutations until they are expressed, neither can it cull out harmful ones until they ultimately find expression. This unfortunate reality creates significant problems for animal breeders who usually need to work with very small populations when cultivating new traits. It has created well-known genetic defects for various breeds of pedigree dogs and cats. We also see significantly higher hereditary problems in very small human populations that have lived in isolated locations for many generations. Most evolutionists claim that speciation occurs in the wild through small populations, which need to be small for any beneficial mutation to become fixed into the population, so it can be built on by subsequent generations. However, the genetic baggage of harmful recessive mutations would also accumulate quite rapidly over time, ultimately resulting in the extinction of all mutant populations due to their lack of fitness for survival. You might ask, how can this be, because the rapid accumulation of destructive mutations would have long ago killed off all life that evolved downstream from the *Cambrian explosion*? Yes, that is an interesting tangent that you may elect to explore![18]

Modern evolutionary theory was built on the premise that beneficial mutations *do* exist, and should be quite *common*. So, what are we to make of the mountain of scientific and medical research into mutations, over the last hundred years, that documents an overwhelmingly destructive pattern in the effects of mutations? Is natural selection able to work many miracles within this destructive trend?

Here is a scenario that might help illustrate the nature of the problem. Imagine you have decided to buy a new car. You go to a reputable car sales company, which has about a hundred new cars in the yard, all in mint condition, their paint gleaming in the early morning sun. The manager calls you and the other customers together, and says that today they have a very special offer. Standing behind him is a bunch of seeming thugs, each holding a sledge hammer. The manager explains that he will let these men run wild in the car yard for half a day. The customer who pays the price of a new vehicle plus a 100 percent surcharge will get the first choice to select the most improved result. The customer who pays the price of new vehicle plus a 90 percent surcharge will be able to select the second most improved result, and so on, down to the customer

18. Google the phrases *Muller's ratchet*, *genetic load*, and *genetic entropy* to explore this topic more deeply.

who pays a 10 percent surcharge who will get to select the tenth most improved result. He then warmly invites you to sign up, and pay in advance, for the package you prefer.

All the scientific and medical evidence indicates that the foundational assumption of frequent beneficial mutations is a myth. Mutations overwhelmingly break, destroy or degrade existing bio-information and the functionality of systems that depend on that information, either at the cellular or organism level. Even selecting the first best from broken remains will still result in something that is significantly inferior to the original. Has scientific and medical research over the last full century confirmed the claim that mutations and natural selection worked together to build the biosphere that we observe? Was that claim a brilliant insight? Or, like the car yard scenario just described, is it completely absurd?

Speciation and Natural Selection

Speciation occurs when a sub-population is isolated from the main population, and gradually develops unique characteristics and genetic differences from the parent population (or other subpopulations that also developed from it), to the extent that its members can no longer produce fertile offspring if interbred with that main population or another subpopulation. Horses and donkeys obviously have a common ancestor, but they are considered to be separate species because the offspring of their interbreeding (mules) are infertile. Lions and tigers can produce offspring together in captivity, but these also are infertile. Purebred domestic dogs or cats may look very different, but they are not considered distinct species because the offspring from interbreeding are all fertile.

The process of domestic breeding and plant cultivation – which theoretically models the mechanisms of speciation but in a much shorter time frame – is not primarily driven by mutations. Some traits, like white sheep with no horns, are indeed the result of mutations.

These mutations have destroyed the ability to grow horns and include melanin in the wool fibres, and provide another illustration of mutations causing a loss of information from the genome. And one can hardly claim the mutants that win some dog and cat shows are better equipped for survival in the wild.

Selective breeding involves the cultivation of lines that possess the desired traits, and terminating those that don't. Yet the majority of those traits come from genetic information that was already present in the parent population, but balanced by other complementary genetic information. Selective breeding culls the genetic information associated with undesirable balancing traits. Domestic purebreds are genetically poorer than their mongrel cousins and ancestors, as owners can easily verify from their accumulating vet bills.

In the wild, natural selection can cull whole populations and subpopulations through extinction. Once information has been culled from a particular domestic line, or subpopulation in the wild, it is gone forever. It is impossible to breed Chihuahua-sized dogs from Great Danes or vice versa. This can only be achieved by cross-breeding, to reintroduce genetic information for new, desired traits. The Irish potato famine in the mid-1800s occurred because their domestic potatoes no longer had genes that gave resistance to potato blight. Scientists and breeders therefore maintain older lines of domestic plants and animals that were recovered from remote locations, where they had been established centuries earlier, in order to preserve valuable genetic information that has been lost from newer lines. Many countries, and the United Nations, have established seed banks – for example, the Svalbard Global Seed Vault in Norway.

The key thing to note is that selective breeding, and speciation or extinctions through natural selection, all result in *loss* of genetic information. They are *downhill* processes, rather than ones that add new genetic information into a population and take it uphill. While bacteria have a built-in mechanism that allows them to exchange short lengths of genetic code, there is no documented evidence to suggest that new genetic information and functionality are actually arising, or are being introduced and fixed into existing wild or domesticated populations. This can happen only through genetic engineering, which currently involves merely inserting genetic information obtained from other species. Extinctions and loss of genetic information is occurring very rapidly – much too rapidly for an evolutionary time frame of hundreds of millions of years. In reality, the 'biosphere ship' is sailing in entirely the opposite direction from the one postulated by evolutionists.

A companion problem is how could evolution frontload the vast amounts of surplus and initially redundant information into the early populations of all modern plant and animal families, which later enabled speciation to proceed? When and why did this occur? Which scenario of origins is most consistent with this reality? Is this another important signpost for us?

Limits to Variation

Selective breeding has revealed an interesting fact: there are limits to genetic variation. Various lines of sugar beet cannot be taken beyond a 14 percent yield. Dogs seem to have already been bred to the limits of variability in size. This is what we could reasonably expect: selective breeding and cultivation cannot take a species beyond the information that already exists within the population. Fruit flies (*Drosophila*) have been used as a source for genetic studies for more than 100 years, especially studies of mutations initiated by X-rays and other forms of radiation which increase mutation rates to thousands of times above normal. These radiation experiments suggest there are also limits to mutations, beyond which the offspring are infertile or not viable at all.

Induced infertility has been used since the 1950s to combat insect plagues, and could potentially be used to fight insect-borne diseases such as the one caused by the Zika virus.[19] While some fear this technique could create a new Frankenstein species, the reality of the destructive nature of mutations has been borne out through the various programmes to date – including successful pioneering work with screw worms in the USA and Mexico from 1951 to 1982.

The limits to variation from mutations may occur because DNA is only half the story. Cell machinery is passed down through the generations from the mother/female without influence from the father/male. This is why geneticists talk about *mitochondrial Eve* and *Y-chromosomal Adam* within humanity. Because sexual reproduction does not affect the cell machinery or the Y chromosome, both of these tend to be very stable, with minimal change across many generations.[20] Infertility or non-viability of the offspring of irradiated fruit flies occurs when excessive mutations to the DNA make it incompatible with the cell machinery in one or more essential functions or, more commonly, damage the control systems that regulate cell differentiation and other sequencing in the early development of their offspring. Current science does not yet fully understand the reasons for these limits to mutational variation. However, it is another example of modern scientific research uncovering serious problems with the evolutionary story.

The fossil record supports this view. After more than 150 years

---

19. There are some problems with using this technique to reduce mosquito populations, because irradiated mosquito males are weakened to the extent that they don't compete well with their wild counterparts.
20. This is why the discovery of the huge differences between the human and chimpanzee Y chromosomes was such a bombshell to those who understood its significance.

of evolution-dominated palaeontological exploration, there is still no evidence that any class or order progressively developed into another. The *missing links* are still conspicuously missing! In this context, the missing links in the fossil record also confirm there are limits to variation.

At this point in our road map we need to address the question: Do the limits to variation that we observe, together with the existence of numerous kingdoms, classes, and orders with no links between them in the fossil record, plus the vast amount of information in the biosphere, all support the evolution story? Or do these additional signposts compel us to consider there is a *very* intelligent designer of all these life forms, and an author of that information?

Life and Biosphere:

Geological Time

The foundational assumption in geology over the last 200 years was, and still is, *gradualism* in the wider context of *uniformitarianism*. This assumption was formulated by James Hutton, Charles Lyell, and others in the late 1700s and early 1800s. It is encapsulated in the mantra that 'the present is the key to the past.' This assumption, in combination with evolutionary assumptions about any fossils they contain, were, and still are, used to estimate the age of geological strata. These dates are now used throughout academic literature, and all geological features are now interpreted within this framework. Radiometric analysis, which is calibrated to these assumptions, is often (understandably) consistent with them. If all these assumptions are correct, then the estimated dates are reasonable. Of course, if some assumptions are flawed, then the dates derived from them will probably be flawed as well.

Following acceptance of the *Missoula flood*(s) in the 1950s,[1]

---

1. J Bretz presented scientific papers in 1923 that postulated a single, massive flood event spanning the states of Montana, Idaho and Washington. However, his controversial conclusions were rejected by the geological community because they were not uniformitarian. In 1942, Joseph Pardee published a paper which identified the source of Bretz's flood event as a massive ice dam that gave way causing the huge lake that had built up behind it to empty very rapidly. Even then, it took a further decade before the Missoula flood was accepted by the scientific community.

there has been mounting evidence that much of the earth's geology has been formed by catastrophic activity. Water flowing at more than 70 km/hr causes cavitation which erodes rocks very rapidly. The Missoula flood, if it was a single event,[2] excavated more than 200 cubic kilometres of sediment, carved out very large valleys, and deposited much of this material over a wide area of ocean floor in a sediment layer that measures up to 500 metres thick in places – all within a few hours!

It is now also known that strata with multiple fine layers form in flood plains during a single flood event, rather than each thin layer taking several millennia as long thought. Most geologists today recognise these realities but have merely accommodated them within the incumbent geological chronology.

However, many homogeneous strata, such as the pure chalk that stretches from Dover to Calais, could not form within gradualistic time frames. The chalk in the English Channel should be mixed with copious amounts of silt and other inorganic sediments, much like the current seabed, if it really accumulated slowly over 35 million years during the Upper Cretaceous period.[3]

The eruption of Mount St Helens in 1980 tragically claimed 57 lives, yet the eruption gave scientists an unsurpassed opportunity to study a catastrophic event of that scale. Forty years on, vegetation is recovering, and wildlife has returned. Many geological features that were created during and immediately after the event look remarkably similar to other features around the world that have been dated as millions of years old.

---

2. There are two schools of thought as to whether the Missoula flood was a single event or not. Many geologists favour a single event. Others advocate up to 40 flood events.
3. Most geologists interpret the Upper Cretaceous as being 60-100 million years ago.

There are many things in the fossil record that are inconsistent with the evolution story. The *missing links* are probably the most well known. Over the last two hundred years, millions of fossils have been excavated and documented. We should expect these to cover all the respective kingdoms with considerable granularity – which they do. However, the granularity is all within the various classes and orders. No transitional fossils have been discovered that demonstrate a development of one phylum, class or order into another. Fossils from respective classes and orders (and families in most cases) just suddenly appear in geological strata. Within families, there is considerable granularity and commonality. So, it is relatively easy to classify species within the same family systematically and, rightly or wrongly, to postulate evolutionary links and lines of development between them and conclude that the similarities are evidence of common descent.

But the links showing how each of the basic classes, orders, and families developed in the first place are still missing from our now extensive documentation of the fossil record. Some may speculate there are more fossils yet to be unearthed (which is true), and that one day we will find many of these missing links. However, given the great volume of fossils that have already been unearthed, is it more reasonable to expect that interesting future finds will merely increase the granularity of the existing picture, rather than fill in the great gulfs between the respective classes and orders? The issue is not that some of the early links are missing, but that *all of them* are missing. There is a bigger picture. These crucial *periods* of evolutionary development are completely missing from the fossil record in their *entirety*. Something is seriously wrong with the fossil record – which undergirds the very foundations of evolution theory.

Living fossils are another oddity in the fossil record. A number of species, thought to be long extinct because they were first discovered as fossils in 'ancient' strata, have turned up alive and well in our current biosphere. Crucially, these modern versions are virtually identical to their fossilised forebears. Examples are the aardvark (found as fossils in the Eocene – thought to be about 55 million years ago), crocodiles (also 55 million years), Coelacanths (found in marine strata dated from 65-80 million years), Wollemi pine (120 million years), maidenhair tree (or Ginkgo biloba: 135 to 210 million years), elephant sharks (up to 420 million years), Horseshoe crabs (450 million years), Nautilus (late Cambrian: 500 million years), and cyanobacteria (which still look the same as those found in Stromatolites that are thought to be 3.5 billion years old).

The challenge posed by living fossils is fairly obvious. How could they have not changed in all that time? Evolutionary theory says that only eight million years is sufficient for an ordinary knuckle-walking ape to transition into a creature that can walk upright – *on the moon*! Stasis over such long periods is explained within the evolutionary paradigm by claiming that the original living-fossil life forms were so well suited to their environment that they did not need to evolve further. Is this sensible? Rapid evolution was supposedly taking place all around them, and giving the evolving species a greater competitive advantage and fitness to survive. Living fossils therefore defy the basic tenets of evolutionary theory. So, are living fossils merely a quirk in the fossil record? Or are they significant clues which suggest that reality is different from what is commonly thought? The alternative – that those fossils and the strata in which they are found can't be that old – is unthinkable for most geologists and palaeontologists.

An interesting article was published in the *New Zealand Herald* on 4 August 2014, in which British scientists Mike Lee and Gareth Dyke stated that there was 'overwhelming evidence that dinosaurs evolved into birds.' They claimed *stem bird* dinosaurs evolved to be smaller in adult size, and it became possible for them to climb trees, eventually developing the ability to glide and then fly. These scientists went on to say that the newly found *Changyuraptor* – a 'feathered dinosaur' with *four* wings, which some scientists date as living 125 million years ago – was obviously a good tree climber because several Changyuraptor fossils have been found with small birds in their stomachs. Excuse me? A stem-bird, which is placed early in the downsizing progression on the branch of the evolutionary tree that eventually led to birds, was feeding on small birds that already existed at that time? The dinosaur-to-bird paradigm is so strong that these two scientists fail to see the contradiction, even though it is in clear view before them.

This is a further example of an evolutionary claim that does not stand up to close scrutiny. Yet, it highlights another inconsistency in the fossil record. 'Younger' fossils are often found in the same strata as 'older' fossils, and rare finds of fossilised stomach contents confirm they coexisted. Flight itself is a missing link with a new twist. Fully functional birds, pterodactyls, changyuraptors, bats, and flying insects all suddenly appear in the fossil record without any ancestors that record their evolutionary development. The evidence that dinosaurs evolved into birds seems instead to be underwhelming.

In 2004, Dr Mary Schweitzer discovered soft tissue in a T-rex femur recovered from Montana's Hell Creek Formation. Scientists had never previously looked for soft tissue in dinosaur fossils because they should be fully mineralised if they are more than 65 million years old. Laboratory experiments demonstrate that soft tissue should completely break down within a few thousand years or, if foreign bacteria are present, in just a matter of weeks. Other scientists then began looking, and have since found soft tissue in many other fossils from all around the world. These finds have three possible explanations: (a) the soft tissue is merely biofilm from recent bacteria; (b) there are unknown mechanisms that can somehow preserve organic molecules for millions of years; or (c) these dinosaur remains are only a few thousand years old. In her subsequent work, Dr Schweitzer identified the protein collagen in this tissue, which invalidated many sceptical claims that this was only recent biofilm.[4]

The evolutionary paradigm demands that some as-yet-unknown mechanism can preserve unfossilised bone, soft tissue, and collagen for more than 65 million years. The alternative, that many dinosaurs lived as recently as only a few thousands of years ago, is axiomatically rejected by most scientists because it would completely upset the applecart. It seems that no one is willing to risk running a carbon-14 analysis of these bone and soft tissue samples which, one way or the other, would bring much-needed, empirical objectivity to the discussion.[5] A group of independent scientists calling themselves The Paleochronology Group have actually conducted carbon-14 analysis of non-fossilised dinosaur bones. They carefully used standard procedures to avoid contamination, and sent 15 samples of interior bone scrapings and fragments from six different dinosaurs to three separate radioisotope-dating laboratories without disclosing their origin. These highly-respected laboratories all returned results with dates ranging from 22,000 to 39,000 years.[6] The academic paper the group then presented at a 2012 geophysics

---

4. 'Collagen has great tensile strength, and is the main component of fascia, cartilage, ligaments, tendons, bone and skin.' (Wikipedia) This protein is very common in animals, but not in bacteria.
5. Carbon-14 can only be used to date things that were alive within the last 60,000 years since it has a short half-life of 5730 years. Beyond that, carbon-14 will decay to the point that it is not detectible. If these dinosaurs are genuinely more than sixty million years old, carbon-14 analysis should obviously register a nil result – if there is no contamination – and confirm that this soft tissue is not recent, as would carbon-14 tests of the bone itself.
6. Retrieved from newgeology.us/presentation48.html

conference in Singapore was subsequently rescinded by the conference organisers, and removed from their website. These researchers have also been blacklisted by the laboratories they used. In science, the normal practice is for other researchers to repeat significant experiments in order to confirm or invalidate the earlier results. In this case, it seems that the establishment has instead closed ranks against these controversial findings. If reality is different from conventional thinking, it would seem that they do not want to know!

Schweitzer is researching possibilities for a preservation mechanism, and has experimental evidence suggesting that iron oxide from decomposed red blood cells could be a candidate. Other scientists are exploring alternative mechanisms. This will be a fascinating field to follow, over the next decade.

However, this episode highlights an important issue. How should we respond when hard scientific data suggests that reality is different from what we understand and expect? Here we have an incumbent paradigm which requires that organic molecules break down at a rate more than ten thousand times slower than we observe with rigorous scientific laboratory experiments. It is possible Schweitzer's research into iron oxide and work by other scientists might find mechanisms that slow chemical breakdown by up to a factor of ten. But is a factor of 10,000 a bridge too far? When one scans the web for scientific literature that discusses the implications of soft tissue being found in dinosaur bones from a significant number of sites around the world, no one within 'the establishment' dares to ask the obvious question. Something is toxic within the culture of the scientific establishment when it suppresses a freewheeling exchange of ideas on this subject, and stifles the humility needed to ask the question, 'Are we seriously mistaken?'

These recent discoveries obviously challenge the foundational assumptions of gradualism and the accuracy of dates based on them. Their implications are profound, and these are understandably very active topics in the creation versus evolution debate. New books are being written regularly on these topics.

Earlier, we discussed Haldane's dilemma, which arose when he attempted to calculate the rate of 'beneficial evolution' and fit the evolutionary development of the current biosphere within the hypothetical upper limit for the age of the earth. We were left in no-man's-land on this, because all such calculations are largely based on hypothetical scenarios and assumptions.

However, the theory of evolution certainly requires deep geological time, and it is a major driver in the setting of our current scientific dates. If geological strata are significantly younger than their claimed ages (even tens of millions rather than hundreds of millions of years old), then evolution would become implausible on this basis alone.

This is a very big topic, with many aspects to consider. In our road map, we can view this subject only in passing. So you may wish to revisit it in due course. It has been included to raise awareness that a number of significant inconveniences have been discovered, over the last few decades, even in the fields of geology and palaeontology.

Life and Biosphere:

A Summary

Hopefully the content of the previous four chapters has given a feel for some of the big boulders in the growing mountain of problems for the theory of evolution. By the same rationale detectives use to eliminate suspects from a list of possibilities, if any one of these boulders is valid then, on its own, it would be sufficient to show up the evolution story as suspect. What would a detective make of *all* the combined evidence? What do we make of it ourselves?

Where are the formal, repeatable, scientific experiments validating the atheistic claims as truly scientific instead of what we now have – unsubstantiated hypothesising that is needed to rescue their philosophy? One needs to apply tests of truth or fiction, and draw some conclusions as to the plausibility of each of the essential atheistic claims which must *all* be true for their theory to hold.

To summarise evolutionist claims:

- Basic chemistry and random motion alone are capable of creating the astonishingly complex nanotechnology of life.
- Matter and energy on their own are able to
  - Create vast amounts of information, and
    - purely random processes can create, rather than destroy, information and could create the huge volume of information essential in the very first cell,

    - purely random processes can also assemble, rather than destroy, highly specific physical structures for the first cell – e.g. a DNA double helix to store the information and the complex matching nanomachinery to read and use it, and
    - beneficial mutations exist, and together with natural selection could overcome genetic load, take things uphill from the first cell, and create the volume of all further information in the entire biosphere.
  - Create the thousands of identical copies of highly complex nanomachines necessary for the first cell to be viable. For one of these machines – ATP synthase – millions of identical copies would be necessary.
  - Write astonishingly sophisticated software that
    - serves as 'firmware' for various nanomachines of life that enables their specific function,
    - contains instructions to build more of them,
    - provides intricate command and control coordination of the thousands of components that are essential within living cells and for the metabolism of whole organisms,
    - governs and enables the highly complex process of cell division, and
    - orchestrates the sequence of seed or embryonic development in myriads of different organisms and higher life forms – including when each part has completed and should be turned off.
  - Create consciousness (see the next section)

- Natural selection can do more than merely cull information from the biosphere through extinction and speciation, which both take the biosphere downhill from an information perspective. It will favour beneficial mutations, thus providing a mechanism for introducing new information into the biosphere and taking it uphill. (The reason we do not observe uphill mutations today is because our observational time frame is too short. Evolution is a process that takes millions of years.)[1]

- Genetic mutations combined with natural selection is a powerful creative force that
  - was the mechanism which created the vast amount of diverse information existing in the biosphere,
  - will, if given enough time, generate all the life forms we observe around us with their enormous array of exquisite design features,
  - can create and orchestrate the huge and highly complex networks of multifaceted, multiple symbiosis that we observe throughout the biosphere, and
  - as we continue to conduct further research, science will eventually uncover and document many irrefutable examples of this, that will demonstrate a general trend taking the modern biosphere uphill.
- 'Enough time' allows random activities to overcome astronomical improbabilities, both in the origin of life itself and in the subsequent generation of all the information that exists in the biosphere.
- Four billion years is enough time to build the biosphere we observe purely through mutations and natural selection.

---

1. Evolutionists seem to pick and choose when and where to apply their mantra: The present is the key to the past.

- The design many perceive in the natural world is merely apparent. (See the later section on this.)

Finally, if we multiply the improbabilities of all the individual components that are essential for a purely naturalistic spontaneous origin of life – the first replicating cell – they equate to winning our electron in the universe lottery trillions of times in a row. The improbability of randomly generating all the information in the entire biosphere is even greater still. It would seem that academia has 'bet the farm' against truly colossal odds, and instructs everyone else to blindly follow their lead. Is that sensible? Those of us who have to live and work in the real world learn the importance of assessing and managing risk, and are entitled to use our own judgement on this issue. From our experience, what level of risk for what level of reward is acceptable for betting, not just the farm, but the entire meaning of life? Is George Wald's mantra that enough time enables the impossible to become possible, and all the thinking that has been built on it, fundamentally flawed? Is it wisdom, or a monstrous folly?

The explosion of knowledge about the chemistry of life and biosphere over the last half-century has provided many objective benchmarks for reliably calibrating our thinking. Do these new discoveries support the evolution story, or do they trigger alarm bells? Are they signposts that point instead to a different reality: that life and the biosphere were created by *someone*?

Consciousness

At this point in our travel guide it would be useful to ponder the wonder of consciousness. What is consciousness? Is it merely a product of highly complex, evolved arrangements of neurons and chemicals as atheism claims? Or do the neurons in the brain provide an interface between a metaphysical component of our human make-up and the physical world – much like computer hardware provides an interface for software?[1] If consciousness is associated with metaphysical dimensions, does it continue in those dimensions after our bodies die?

Deterioration of the brain, due to Alzheimer's or dementia, certainly affects a person's memory, personality and ability to respond to their environment – which is consistent with the atheistic claim. However, it is also consistent with a metaphysical source of consciousness in much the same way as a faulty mouse, keyboard or screen connection inhibits a computer program's interface with its environment, or a faulty memory chip or hard drive adversely impacts the ability of software to work correctly. So the effects of these awful conditions are consistent with both perspectives. In the heart-wrenching setting of a hospital intensive care ward, the body

---

1. While computer hardware can be very complex in itself, it is completely useless without appropriate software.

of a person can be kept alive on a life-support unit after their brain has 'died'. This is also consistent with both perspectives. Thus, unfortunately, our current medical experience cannot give us an indication as to which view of consciousness is closer to reality.

A few years ago, I watched a TV documentary where a futurist claimed that by about 2030 we would be able to transfer human personality into a newly cloned, but younger, body when the old one was about to die. This is like restoring a backup of your software and data into a new computer when your old one is about to expire. While the futurist might be commended for his optimism, it seems he seriously underestimated the complexity of our human make-up and the technical difficulty of reading the vast three-dimensional network between neurons, which plays an important role in the mechanism by which memories are stored in our brains. Even if we could do this, would it be enough? Is consciousness (the 'real' us) merely a collection of three-dimensional links between neurons, as materialistic philosophy insists? If it involves an essence that transcends this physical world, how would one identify, represent, and contain this in a physical backup – let alone restore it into a newly cloned body? The futurist also assumed that a newly cloned body would not be already occupied, in contrast to what occurs when foetal cells naturally clone themselves into an identical twin, and to what has been observed of cloned animals.

We regularly hear claims that in another 10 to 20 years computers will have grown in complexity and computational speed to the extent that they will achieve 'artificial consciousness'.[2] However,

---

2. In an article, researcher Andrew Sheehy is reported to have stated that 'although the thinking behind machine consciousness can create issues with the belief of humankind and spirituality … it's "just another phase in the evolution of the human species." The consensus among supporters on when machine consciousness will be achieved is between 10 and 20 years.'

there are many other scientists, engineers, and philosophers who claim that even in 100 years' time computers will still be only machines and, as such, will never achieve sentience, nor awareness of their own existence, let alone sapience. Who is correct? When you read more deeply, some in the first camp are merely talking about mimicked or apparent consciousness. Therefore, to some extent both camps are talking at cross purposes, because they use different definitions of consciousness.

So, we go back to the first question: What exactly is consciousness? A companion question is: What is life? What distinguishes, say, my family's pet rabbit – which regularly hops over to me and waits to be picked up and stroked – from a fluffy robot that can mimic this behaviour? One obvious distinction is the complexity of what lies beneath the fluffy exterior. For starters, robotic rabbits will probably never be fully self-contained to the extent that they have the ability to reproduce. And it may be a few hundred years before human technology enables robotic rabbits to power themselves from grass instead of batteries. However, let's come back to sentience and consciousness. While atheistic philosophy dictates otherwise, it is fairly obvious to many of us that there is a metaphysical component to consciousness, which irreversibly departs when a higher life form, even such as a rabbit, dies. Furthermore, the capacity of humans for abstract understanding and reasoning takes this to another level again.

Consciousness is similar to information in that it is obviously not a property of any of the raw materials of this universe – protons, electrons, atoms, molecules, photons, or energy – or even a direct derivative of the laws of physics and chemistry. So what is it? Where did it come from? Does the evolutionary story offer

---

Retrieved from www.dailymail.co.uk/sciencetech/article-2635011/Google-create-CONSCIOUS-computer-expert-claims.html

plausible explanations for its origin? Or have atheists dictated very simplistic and unsubstantiated claims to us, then taken this issue off the table? Is consciousness another signpost that points to a creator who has spiritual dimensions, and to a world beyond this physical space-time universe?

Design – Apparent or Real?

When many people look at the universe and biosphere, they see 'design' written all over them – which, for them, implies a designer. However, atheists tell us that this is only 'apparent design'. They say that given enough time, stars, galaxies, and planets like Earth will form all by themselves after a big bang. They also claim that, when given enough time, atoms will organise themselves to create life, and genetic mutations coupled with natural selection would then be able to create fully functional flowers, legs, wings, eyes, and ecosystems – and brains that can write and read a book like this, and understand the abstract concepts it contains. Which view is closer to the real truth?

This is not a simple matter because different philosophical camps view the same objective reality from behind the bridge of their own nose. Evolutionists tend to see all changes over time as examples of evolution. For example, my son's Year 13 biology textbook[1] cites several losses of functionality (e.g. blind fish in caves and flightless birds) as being evidence *for* uphill evolution. Creationists will see the same changes as examples of a ubiquitous downhill trend. Evolutionists also see commonalities as proof of common descent

---

1. Hanson, M. (2013). *Excellence in Biology NCEA Level 3,* (pp. 197-199). Sydney, Australia: Cengage Learning. This is the standard textbook for all state schools in New Zealand.

– or of convergent evolution for unique commonalities found in only some species within different taxonomic orders. Creationists see commonalities as examples of common design.

My son's biology textbook also has a subsection entitled Comparative Anatomy, within a larger section called Evidence for Evolution. This text cites the similarities in the pentadactyl limb skeleton across several taxonomical orders – including mole claws, human hands, bat wings, and dolphin flippers – as evidence of common descent. There is no acknowledgement that the similar bone structures are very sensible from a design perspective as they enable large movement, large rotation, and fine control of the tips. Conspicuous differences are also sensible from a design perspective, in that animals such as the horse, sheep, and pig have a single bone (where a human arm has two), because this prevents large rotation of the legs, which would reduce their strength and create unnecessary risk of twisting injuries. Their simpler bone structure at the tips is also ideal as there is little need for fine control of hooves. My son's textbook claims that these differences are fully explained as 'greatly modified by fusion, loss or, in the case of whales, multiplication of bones.'[2] In a tone of complete infallibility, the book teaches students that the single bone in a horse's leg was once two bones that have now fused back into one. This is pure conjecture, driven by philosophy, rather than objective science; there is no fossil evidence whatsoever that demonstrates such a development sequence. We can all convince ourselves that we are right, if we are unwilling to consider other possibilities.

In the section headed The Universe, I suggested that the claim the earth as we find it could form all by itself is beyond the bounds of probability, and even defies various laws of physics. The earth

2. Hanson, p. 197.

as we find it seems to be full of design features that suggest genuine design rather than apparent design, and which are probably intended to serve as signposts for us. If everything was created, then it is sensible to conclude that the design we see is genuine engineering design, and that the Creator probably always intended it should be recognised as such, and point every generation towards him, the designer.

This is a crucial matter, because it determines our interpretation of the natural world around us, and therefore our perception of reality and truth itself. If the atheistic claim of apparent design is correct, then this is a brilliant piece of counter-intuitive insight. It is counter-intuitive because no sophisticated system in human experience has the *appearance* of design and yet had no intelligence involved in that design.[3] However, if this atheistic claim is wrong, then it is a heinous, recklessly erroneous view that has deceived many people, and blinded them to the signposts which could have helped them seek and connect with their Maker. We should go even further than this: If it is wrong, it would be a monstrous evil that has deliberately and wilfully turned those signposts around, so they point in the opposite direction, preventing literally hundreds of millions of people from finding their way home.

One fascinating aspect of nature is the many symbiotic relationships that occur. Some are quite simple relationships between two different species, such as cleaner fish and the larger fish they service at their 'cleaning stations'. Simple relationships like these can be explained relatively easily within an evolutionary framework.

---

3. Atheists might point to something like the water cycle on earth as an example of a system that requires no intelligence. But this is actually circular reasoning (no pun intended), which does not take everything into account. Theists, in turn, claim that several critical aspects of the water cycle reflect clever design.

The biosphere has many essential components, from the humble bacteria at the very bottom of the food chain all the way up to flowering and fruiting plants, insects, and higher birds and animals. There are many complex networks of relationships between multitudes of life forms and kingdoms, and there would be dire consequences if some of them did not exist – such as earthworms, or the bacteria that work symbiotically with nitrogen-fixing plants. Could the entire biosphere we observe today really have 'pulled itself up by the bootstraps' from a single original bacterium?

We need to probe the credibility of the atheistic claim that we see 'only the appearance of design'. A useful question to ask ourselves is, 'How could completely mindless and random processes produce a world that has the appearance of design rather than the appearance of randomness and chaos?' The atheistic claim runs completely contrary to our own objective experience of random processes at work in the real world. The interplay of information and nanomachinery within living cells, and the control systems within organisms, exhibit colossal complexity and exquisite organisation. If we remove our philosophical spectacles, can we think of even one indisputable example where random processes have produced as much as a simple functional system?

To assess the atheistic claims about the biosphere, we simply need to ask the question: Can we realistically expect the plethora of wonderful, biological innovations to have arisen *all by themselves* through a continuous succession of generations with minute incremental changes that natural selection would favour? Its companion question is this: Realistically, are there any biological innovations that *could not* have arisen through a continual sequence of favourable minute changes? If the answer to the first is no, or is yes to the second, then the atheistic claims are neither credible nor sensible.

So, at this point of our road map, let's further assess the plausibility of the atheistic axiom that every scientific observation reflects merely apparent rather than real design. Almost everything within the cosmos and biosphere has the appearance of design. However, for the sake of brevity, we need to narrow this discussion to just a few of the big ones. Consider these points again, but this time from a design perspective:

- The combined improbability of the fine-tuning of the universe
- The combined improbability of all the goldilocks factors of planet Earth

Then, considering the nanotechnology within living cells and, by implication, the hypothetical first cell, again from a design perspective:

- Could the entire first cell's machinery really be assembled through random motion? Or does that machinery indicate real design *and* implementation? What about:
  - The complex and *precise* arrangements of molecules within the many machines,
  - The need for many identical copies of these machines for viability – at least a thousand ribosomes, and millions of ATP synthase,
  - The various cellular systems that require multiple machines, for example RNA polymerase, ribosomes, chaperones, and chaperonins which are all essential components in the manufacture of enzymes, which are in turn essential for the basic chemistry of the cell to work,
  - The optimal design of the coding system of DNA and its match with the transcription machinery,

- The structure of DNA itself. Could it really be formed by random molecular motion? What do laboratory experiments demonstrate in this regard?
- The sheer volume of information that is stored in the DNA and the dependency of the various cell machines on their matching DNA 'firmware',
- The improbability of all this information having come together by random chance, and
- How could the first cell have been powered up to the energy state (i.e. much ATP in its cytoplasm) that enabled the machinery of life to start working? Could natural processes do this, or does it indicate not only design, but also implementation by an external agent?

• Is the claim that mutations can combine with natural selection to create vast amounts of new information true, or is it a philosophically driven fantasy? It can only be one or the other. Was all the information in the biosphere that we clearly observe produced by this mechanism or not? What do the mathematical properties of information, and our own experience of information suggest in this regard? If this claim is a myth, then the design implications of bioinformation are deafening.

It might also be helpful to assess systematically whether any, or all, of the following could have been achieved by contiguous sequences of minute changes or mutations, over many generations, that were all favoured, rather than culled, by natural selection. We should pay close attention to the hypothetical early stages, before any actual positive functionality could realistically be achieved:

• Cell division: The activity of many cellular components

during cell division is very different from a cell's normal operation. The DNA is split into two separate strands which are then reconstructed into two separate double helices. These must then be physically moved so that one copy is located in each half that is formed by the restructured cell membrane (which is also growing and reforming in a way that is very different from its normal operation). The entire process is colossally complex, and requires deft timing and coordination. How could the first cell have possessed the necessary software and matching machinery responses for cell division, over and above all the complex essentials to be viable on its own?

- Limbs: These would have required complex, simultaneous developments in the skeleton, muscles and neural system, and would provide no selective advantage until they had developed, over many generations, to the size and degree of coordination that provided some useful functionality.

- Flight: This requires many special design features that on their own would create a disadvantage until they were combined with several other special features so that a modicum of flight was possible.

- Vision: Evolution theory hypothesises that vision began with a single non-directional photoreceptor. This progressively developed into the compound eyes of the insect kingdom and the high-resolution capabilities found in birds, animals, and fish. The first hypothetical eye would require simultaneous introduction of the photoreceptor's chemistry and structure, a neural pathway to the brain, and cognitive ability within the brain. This, in turn, would require tens of thousands of mutually complementing beneficial mutations.

Is that a sensible proposition, especially given what we know about the destructive nature of mutations? There are many different design schemes for vision in the biosphere, some of which are so incompatible that they would require completely independent evolutionary pathways. Could that many different schemes for vision realistically have evolved independently?

- Other senses: Smell is particularly challenging. It requires special apparatus that can detect very small traces of complex molecules and, again, the neural-cognitive ability to discern, interpret, and respond to them. The abilities of many insects and animals are quite remarkable in this regard.
- Metamorphosis: This is a feature of both the insect and amphibian kingdoms. There is a problem here which should not be understated. The control systems for successfully transforming one body plan into a completely different one are phenomenally complex. In the insect kingdom it is even more problematic, because the cocoon stage is not a self-sufficient life form.[4] Is it credible that each of the examples we observe today could have been achieved purely through a sequence of millions of incremental changes that always resulted in a viable and fertile second life form? Is it credible that this could have been achieved even once in a common ancestor to all insects?

---

4. The biochemistry and control systems within an insect cocoon or chrysalis are truly astonishing. Many of the cells are completely broken down into a basic 'chemical soup', and many new cells for the new adult are assembled from scratch reusing these raw materials from the original caterpillar. We should allow ourselves to ask: are claims that this process could develop incrementally over many generations rooted in reality?

- At what point would the baton for reproduction be passed from the first body plan to the next, and what would be the survival advantage of the second body plan until it had?
- Is it sensible for evolutionary 'fit' and successful caterpillars to continually experiment with transforming themselves into a very different life form with all the special features necessary for flight? Would natural selection all the while favour the progression over many generations before flight was finally achieved?
- Conversely, is it sensible to assume that natural selection would allow a flying insect (such as a praying mantis, which does not undergo metamorphosis) to 'experiment' with alternative juvenile forms until it had successfully developed one that was fitter – because it could feed on a totally different food source, then turn itself into a flying adult?
- Or is it even sensible for some hypothetical ancestor that was neither a caterpillar nor a flying insect to evolve incrementally into a new life form with a dual body plan encoded in its DNA, together with intricate control systems for transforming viably from one to the other?
- All the above scenarios seem to completely contradict the tenets of current evolutionary dogma: that all innovations are merely the product of mindless mutations accumulated over thousands of generations, facilitated by natural selection. While recent research and current knowledge have exponentially increased our understanding of the inner workings of metamorphosis, the problems it posed were obvious even at the time that Darwin wrote *On the Origin of Species*. Are those who

insist that the exquisite design in metamorphosis is merely apparent design being honest and objective? Or does their underpinning philosophy cause them to wilfully ignore an implied *real* design?

- Moulting: This is the mechanism by which insects, spiders, scorpions, and crustaceans periodically shed their exoskeleton as they grow.[5] It involves completely severing *all* chemical and physical bonds with the old skeleton, and developing (and lubricating) a soft, second membrane inside their existing skeleton. It also involves an astonishing feat of coordination – involving new programs in the neural system – that enables them to create an opening in the old skeleton in the appropriate place, and extract themselves from it through this opening. Extracting their jointed limbs makes this process even more remarkable. They then need the temporary ability to move around with only a soft skeleton, and to grow their new, larger exoskeleton quickly. Like metamorphosis, moulting is an all-or-nothing activity. It has no viable, incremental pathway. What would drive many consecutive generations of their respective, hypothetical ancestors to continue experimenting until one of them eventually pulled this off? Do we observe anything in the biosphere today that demonstrates species experimenting like this? Is it sensible to believe that species might have engaged in such experimentation in the past? Such experimentation flies in the face of evolutionary theory – natural selection would work against it.

5. YouTube has several brilliant video clips of this process for various species.

- The three-way symbiotic relationships between whole kingdoms: Many flowering plants are dependent on insects for their fertilisation. Equally, insects are dependent on flowers for their food source. The flowering plants embed their seeds in fruit which ripen at the same time as the seeds become ready (and not before), such that they become attractive to birds and animals who then unwittingly distribute the seeds. Birds especially are almost completely dependent on the other two kingdoms for their food supply, and they are the best distributors of seeds. Many plants seem specially designed for birds to be the main distributors. Modern observational science is beginning to understand some of the intricate control systems for flowers and fruiting, insect development, and flight in both birds and insects. Consider the credibility of the atheistic claims that the mutually dependent flower, insect, and bird kingdoms could simultaneously develop, when each were dependent on the simultaneous development of their partners in this three-way symbiosis. What thresholds of development would be necessary before one of these kingdoms was compatible with, and useful to, the other two kingdoms? What would drive the mutualistic development of all three kingdoms until then?

- In reality, the symbiotic relationships within various ecosystems are far more complex than the three-way symbiosis just described. Every distinct ecosystem around the planet involves whole networks of interdependence. The failures of Biosphere 2 indicate that ecosystems are not as robust as evolutionary axioms require. During the two years it ran, more than 75 percent of its small vertebrates became extinct, as did almost all the insect species, including those which had been chosen for the purpose of pollinating plants. The growth of some species – ants, cockroaches, and katydids – was rampant, and certain vines would have choked out almost every other kind of plant if the human occupants had not intervened.[6] Do our many modern-day experiences with biosecurity breaches also challenge simplistic evolutionary claims? Would rampant, self-serving, survival-of-the-fittest evolution really build balanced ecosystems, or would it rapidly denude the planet of biodiversity – and ultimately all life. Is it reasonable to claim that random activity over time would do a better job than the modern, big-budget scientific planning of Biosphere 2? Would evolution really produce such diverse and stable ecosystems, or does what we observe of various, distinct ecosystems all around the planet, reflect real and extremely intelligent design – and perhaps management.

- The colossal complexity and capability of the human brain and psyche: The size of a human's memory and our mathematical, engineering, and artistic abilities are truly amazing. We seem to be hugely over-endowed to be mere products of random mutations and survival-of-the-fittest natural selection. Lions and wolves have sufficient social order to hunt in packs without communication through language. Why, and how, did humans develop the physical and neural attributes essential for language, along with all its complex grammatical structures? Interestingly, most ancient languages had grammar structures that were significantly more complex than modern ones – which is even harder to explain

---

6. Some of the material referred to here is from biology.kenyon.edu/slonc/bio3/2000projects/carroll_d_walker_e/whatwentwrong.html

> within an evolutionary paradigm. How did evolutionary mechanisms endow humans with redundant mathematical abilities, which then enabled the engineering and scientific achievements of the last few thousand years? Many human characteristics seem to be specifically designed to let us enjoy the world around us and allow us to live harmoniously in community. Why does music resonate so deeply in our human psyche? Why, and how, did survival of the fittest produce that? Why do we appreciate beauty (with all our senses, including smell and touch), from natural wonders, through art works, to pleasant human faces? What is the survival advantage of this? It seems to be a distraction from evolutionary purposes. One must resort to some very long, thin, hypothetical storytelling to accommodate many human attributes within an atheistic framework.

Which of the above fit comfortably within the evolutionary paradigm? Those that do not are conspicuous signposts, that point to genuine design by an astonishing intellect – and creative genius.

At this point on our road map we need to assess the credibility of the atheistic axiom that the vast design that many readily perceive in the cosmos, earth, and biosphere is merely an 'apparent' design that is ultimately an illusion. Weigh this against the alternative view, that all three of these exhibit real design, and provide many genuine signposts pointing to a very intelligent and innovative designer. The design found throughout the natural world is often astonishingly exquisite. Is this observation more consistent with the claim that the cosmos and biosphere are the handiwork of an extraordinary designer, or the claim that they are merely the product of blind evolutionary mechanisms that are still in the process of upgrading the biosphere from very rudimentary beginnings? When we look, with open minds, at many aspects of the biosphere especially, there would seem to be numerous examples of genuine design quietly staring back at us. Is all this design merely 'apparent' – or is it very real?

Scientific Laws

We should contemplate the essence and importance of the laws of physics, chemistry, mathematics, and information – and their implications for this subject. If I announced I was going to pour a bucket of water on my driveway and then push every last drop all the way from there up to the top of Mount Everest using only a rake, people, with good reason, would think I was stupid. If, despite reasoned objections, I insisted I could do it given enough time, my family and close friends would try to persuade me to have a psych assessment. The laws of physics would work against my achieving such a goal, and make the task impossible within milliseconds. The scientific laws governing evaporation and the capillary attraction of water molecules to concrete would make the probability of success if given enough time the same as the probability of success in 'not much time at all'. In this scenario, these probabilities are both significantly less than miniscule. They are absolutely zero!

With considerable intelligence and engineering effort, we can employ some scientific laws to prevail over others – enabling an aircraft to leave the runway, or food to be stored safely in a freezer for several months. However, all these laws allow us to make robust predictions as to how matter and energy will behave if left to itself. They define clear empirical boundaries beyond which things genuinely are impossible. Therefore, these laws provide reliable benchmarks against which we can objectively assess various claims about origins.

Many atheistic assertions for a naturalistic origin of the cosmos, life and the biosphere are in essence philosophical views. These assertions are not supported *consistently* by scientific observations because they defy one or more of the foundational laws of matter, energy, and information in some way, and far exceed reasonable expectations of statistical mathematics. The claimants seem to hustle these problems quickly into the undergrowth. Of course, the creation of everything by an almighty God also defies every scientific law that has ever been identified. However, this alternative does at least give a plausible reason for this – that is, plausible to those who are open to such a possibility.

We cannot reconcile a number of natural laws which have been scientifically documented – such as the laws of thermodynamics and momentum, and some laws of chemistry and information – with a purely naturalistic origin of the cosmos and biosphere we observe. Several significant rules of statistical mathematics have been inexplicably overcome during the origin of the cosmos, life, and the biosphere. A large element of faith is required to fit what we observe into any philosophical framework. Creationists obviously have faith that the cosmos and biosphere were created by an infinite and eternal being who inhabits other dimensions beyond the creation. Perhaps atheists have an even stronger faith: they believe that evolution is a fact, that all the design that others perceive around them is merely 'apparent', and that one day science will discover answers to all the problems that have been created by recent observations. Have we reached the summit of the mountain of problems, such that many answers will now fall into place for evolution theory? Or will further research only cause the mountain's rate of growth to continue its escalating trend?

The issue of origins confronts us with a dilemma which, due to its very nature, cannot be resolved from within the confines of observational science because the conclusions are dependent on the philosophical framework we use to interpret those observations. Therefore, the 'facts' don't necessarily speak for themselves. We can either cut our losses with a naturalistic story that is at least consistent with some natural laws while ignoring other laws of physics, chemistry, statistics, and information that are problematic for various aspects of that story. Or we can accept something like the biblical account at face value, or perhaps develop our own compromise somewhere between these two boundaries.

These are the claims that need to be assessed against the benchmark of Scientific Law:

- Does the claim that all the matter and energy in the universe somehow created itself out of nothing through self-contained naturalistic processes fall within or beyond the empirical boundary defined by the laws of thermodynamics?
- Does the claim that free amino acids in a primordial soup polymerised using peptide bonds into full length protein molecules lie inside or beyond a numeric boundary that is similarly defined by the laws of thermodynamics?
- Is this empirical boundary confirmed experimentally by formal observations of the behaviour of free amino acids in a laboratory flask today?
- Is the claim that random activity could create the genome of the first cell consistent with the laws of information?
- Do the compounding improbabilities in the naturalistic story for the origin of life fall within or beyond boundaries set by the laws of statistical mathematics?
- Is it consistent with the laws of mathematics to claim that natural selection once had the ability to transform the

negative totals of accumulating mutations into positive numbers?

Every philosophical framework has a creation story. If we were able to step outside our own framework and view them all objectively, which framework's creation story best harmonises *all* our currently documented scientific laws with *all* our current observations about the cosmos and biosphere? The tests of truth demand that we should not cherry-pick just the observations that are convenient to our own current framework. Which framework best explains the very existence of the laws themselves and how they were suspended during the origins process? Does any creation story pass every test of truth that we can humbly ask of it?

The implications of natural laws are obvious, and should be considered at this point in our road map as we carefully evaluate and choose between competing philosophical frameworks. The philosophical framework that is most scientific is not necessarily the one that is held by the most scientists. It is the one that best conforms to all established scientific laws and observations. Various paradigm shifts in the history of science provide good evidence of this. Is our commitment to truth such that we are prepared to revise our current interpretive framework objectively, in the bright light of the laws of science? We are all inclined to instinctively answer 'yes, of course' to such a question. So perhaps we should also ask ourselves, on a scale of zero to 10, how truthful was our answer?

Conclusion to Origins

We are like people living in the valley below a dam that has just been built. A land and housing boom began when the intention to build a dam was first announced, and many new people are still moving into the valley. During its planning phase and construction, a number of independent engineers warned that the dam had serious design flaws, and these engineers persist with their warnings. Nevertheless, the dam's designers, contractors, and the local authority all insist that the design and construction are sound. Recently, rumours have been circulating that hairline cracks have started to appear, as the water level behind the dam has risen; not just a few cracks, but lots of them, all over the dam. The designers and local council insist that there are no problems, and that the dam will pass the test of the water reaching its maximum level, and serve the community well for many decades. They also make frequent statements in the local media to affirm this, and to discredit the engineers ringing alarm bells and the people spreading the rumours. We don't have the technical or logistical ability to inspect the dam first-hand ourselves, and are not sure who to believe. Many people trust the local authorities implicitly and, because they have performed well in many other areas, we are inclined to trust them in this matter also. We have read several open letters from engineers who have concerns, and their concerns sound quite reasonable. How should we respond? We can take a 'she'll be right' approach, and carry on being preoccupied with our busy lives. But the stakes are high and, as loving and responsible parents, concerns for the safety of our children often niggle us. What would happen if the dam catastrophically failed while our children were at school? The school board is so confident of the official line that it won't conduct any investigation of its own, and refuses to undertake even the most basic contingency planning, of drawing up a rapid evacuation plan?

Faced with such a scenario, most of us would start to do our own private research, and to discuss the subject with one or two people we knew who were similarly concerned, and who had the ability to discern between fact and fiction. We would be diligent about this, and if our research deepened our concern rather than alleviating it, we would consider selling up and moving out of the valley.

Our understanding of origins is more of a high-stakes issue than many people realise. Wrong understanding in this matter strikes at the jugular of the meaning of life. Time itself will eventually expose the difference between truth and fiction on this issue too. However, life is short. Given how long the debate has been running, and the entrenched views held by some key players, we cannot wait for it to play out to its own conclusion. We need to take the same approach with the subject of origins as we would if faced with the dam scenario.

As the theory of evolution was gaining traction in the late 1800s, several prominent scientists, like Louis Pasteur, opposed it based on genuine experimental evidence. We should regularly remind ourselves that any incorrect starting assumptions will predetermine our reaching wrong conclusions. Over the last half-century scientific research has uncovered many new and serious problems for atheistic assumptions and naturalistic theories of origins. Yet these assumptions and theories are still currently held in academia, taught in our education systems, and frequently presented by the media. There is an elephant in the room – a very large one at that. These problems continue to be dismissed and ridiculed by many influential scientists and educationalists who hold key positions within the establishment, and this dismissive attitude has been adopted by our whole society. No one is asking the useful questions often asked in boardrooms in both the engineering profession and wider business world: What are we overlooking? What if we are wrong?

Research over the next decade and beyond will discover many more fascinating layers of complexity in the cosmos, in molecular biology, and in the biosphere. These findings will raise the bar for naturalistic origins by many more orders of magnitude – at an even faster rate than over the last decade. Each of us must face a question that probes the depth of our own intellectual integrity, especially if we continue to hold to the status quo. The question is: At what point does the level of the bar become too high for me? This naturally leads to a second question: Have we reached that point already?

Will the theory of evolution pass the test of time, or does it have a use-by date? If the accumulation of inconvenient discoveries continues to follow the escalating trend of the last 50 years, we will reach a point where the interpretive tide turns. Are we approaching a paradigm shift? Will our children or grandchildren's generation view us and the last 150 years of 'origins science' as having embraced a great folly, and struggle to understand both how and why we fell for it? If we are seriously mistaken in this issue, do we really want to know? Is the theory of evolution a brilliant insight, or is it the biggest bungle in the history of science? Is it time to think again?

Hopefully this half of the book has been both informative and helpful. It may have stimulated further investigation of these issues. At this point in the road map you may wish to draw some tentative conclusions which, in turn, will affect the direction your journey now takes. I trust the next section will help you even further.

PART TWO

Thinking Again: If We Are Created

Sifting Through the Alternatives

The First Fork in the Road

There are only two possible explanations for the existence of the universe and biosphere: either they came into being of their own accord by purely self-contained natural processes, or they were caused (created) by something, or someone, outside the system. So, we have a clear either/or choice at this point in our road map. Are we here through natural causes, or were we created?

Is what we observe here in the 21st century consistent with our legacy of atheistic and evolutionary philosophy from the mid-1800s? Or have we come full circle to where we can acknowledge that ancient humankind may have been closer to the truth about our origins than we were in our over-simplistic nineteenth and twentieth century presumption?[1]

Upon reflection, you may find yourself in no man's land. You have been bombarded with atheistic views all your life, through the education system, media, books, and even speakers you have heard.

---

1. It is easy to dismiss the views of earlier generations out of a mistaken sense of superiority. Through over-simplification and stereotyping, we can under-estimate the diversity within any given generation and fail to recognise that much went on in them that has been lost with time. And we can easily overlook the fact that technical knowledge is not the same as wisdom.

Could all of them have been mistaken? If evolution is the worst bungle in the history of science, then you may need time to process the enormity of this. You might even need to go back and re-read some of the earlier sections, and do further research of your own.[2]

But if you have concluded that what we observe of the universe and biosphere is more consistent with their having been created by a super-intelligent, super-energetic, and super-capable architect or engineer, then your road map is only just beginning. What is this designer like? Much of what we observe, especially of the nanotechnology of life, reflects indescribable engineering ability, which in turn reflects deep underlying goals, purpose, and implementation planning. For what purpose was the world and universe around us created? Has the master engineer or Creator communicated with humankind?

Such questions can take many of us outside our comfort zone. Our close friends and family may not be interested in them at all, and exploring them on our own may be quite daunting. Over the years, we acquire humility, awareness, and caution. This usually accumulates from experiences where reality proved more complex than our initial, simplistic expectations. In many situations it is easy to overlook quite significant factors that totally change the outcome. There is a healthy balance between not trusting ourselves to act independently, and having the courage to embrace the truth we discover, even if it takes us into unexplored territory. This road map will guide you to important questions and considerations, so you can explore them with greater confidence. But it is limited by pragmatic constraints on time and content length. Hopefully, it

---

2. Useful resources: www.wikipedia.org provides overviews of most topics – usually from a pro-evolution perspective – and relevant external links. Useful sites that present the creation perspective are: creation.com, icr.org, and crev.info.

opens out the big questions systematically, and helps to identify things you may wish to explore in greater depth.

The realisation that we and the universe around us were created is a huge watershed. It throws a completely different light on everything, and provides a very different framework for understanding the world around us – and life itself. The calibre of the design that can be perceived everywhere in the natural world, indicates that its creator has colossal intelligence and planning ability. This in turn strongly suggests that life has meaning, and we can start to ask what that meaning is. It also raises an important question: Can we 'find our way home' to the one who made us?

Has the Creator Since Died?

This suggestion has been mooted by various people in the past in one of two forms: either the Creator kick-started primordial life and evolutionary processes, or he created everything almost as we now see it, and then left us to it.

If we have already concluded that evolutionary theory is a myth, then the first variant is not tenable. While the second variant might be more feasible, we should ask ourselves if it is even possible for the Creator to die? Is death an event that applies only to life forms that are dependent on chemistry, information, and external energy for their existence?

This question cannot be resolved at this point in our road map. It is probably best answered by encountering first-hand evidence that God is still alive and well. Therefore, this must wait until farther into our journey.

(Preview: If death is an event that is only applicable to life-forms that are dependent on chemistry and external energy, then what implications does this have for us and the duration of 'life beyond death', if that will no longer require a physical body?)

Spaghetti Junction

If we accept that this universe could not have created itself out of nothing and needed intelligence in its design, and therefore that 'God' exists, it immediately raises the question, has the Creator attempted to communicate with humankind, and perhaps even given us a 'Maker's handbook'? This question quickly leads us to a very confusing junction, with many paths leading away from it in different directions.

There are many different religions in this world. Do they all ultimately lead to the same place, as Baha'i tell us? This sounds very nice and tolerant, and it doesn't offend anyone. But is it true? Hinduism's reincarnation and nirvana, Buddhism's nirvana, New Age's human essence, and the Jewish/Christian/Muslim concept of having one life and then giving account for it before our Maker, all seem to be very different final destinations. They are so different from each other that they can't *all* be true. After 'giving account', Islam's promise of perpetual hedonism contradicts some of Mohammed's teaching for conduct in this life. Further, Islam's concept is obviously a very different destination from that of Christianity and Judaism, which both anticipate being in the presence of an infinitely loving, wise, and *holy* God – and a very different ecstasy, flowing from involvement in his vast purposes for the rest of eternity. Where is clarity to be found?

Which Way Is Up?

At this point it would be good to step back for a moment and consider what the creation suggests about the nature and attributes of its creator. That will set a benchmark against which we can assess the credibility of the various paths presented to us. Those paths, which don't match this benchmark, should not be allowed to occupy our time and delay us from the most promising path. We have the advantage of 21st century science to calibrate our benchmarks, whereas ancient authors had no such insight to influence what they wrote. Statements about the creation and Creator that were way ahead of their time probably indicate that the authors had outside help to write what they did.

So, let's take another look at the universe and biosphere around us, but this time for the purpose of identifying some key attributes of the entity that created them:

- The universe is vast; its dimensions stretch to infinity. So, the Creator must be very 'big' too. In fact, the infinite nature of the dimensions of the universe strongly suggests that whoever made it must also be infinite.

- I remember reading a news article about hurricane Yasi that hit Queensland in January 2011. It said that a Category 5 hurricane like Yasi had enough energy to power the world for a year. That energy came from sunlight warming a relatively small area of the Pacific Ocean over a few weeks. Just imagine how much energy arrives on the entire earth from the sun over a full year. The relative proportions of our solar system are such that, if the sun was the size of a regulation basketball, Earth would be like a 2 mm ball-bearing about 21 metres[3] away. Now imagine that you are the sun, looking out to a planet with a relative size like a small ball-bearing about 21 metres away. How much *more* energy is radiating out from you than the amount that warms the earth? (If you want to know, it is 2.4 billion times more,

---

3. For American readers: 2 mm is about 0.08 inch, and 21 metres is about 23 yards

if my calculations are correct.) Now consider the amount of energy radiating from the 200 billion stars of our Milky Way galaxy. Finally, ponder the amount of energy that currently radiates from the 100 billion galaxies of the known universe in just one year. This Creator has energy to burn…

- The laws of physics, mathematics, and other general laws of nature are all very consistent and logical. (Well, quantum mechanics, sub-atomic physics, and general relativity get a bit weird, but they are at least coherent.) This strongly suggests that the Creator is logical, consistent, and sensible. In fact, this was the foundational premise that led to modern science.

- The inner workings of the cell and human brain indicate that the Creator has vast engineering ability that can conceive, plan, coordinate, and implement extremely minute details and the extensive network of four-dimensional relationships between them – many of those relationships also involve time. This in turn reflects immeasurable intelligence. It also reflects infinitely detailed control of his creation, in order to build (and perhaps sustain) such systems, including the minute nanotechnology of life and balance of ecosystems.

- The Creator seems to really enjoy diversity. Consider the uniqueness of every star, planet, moon, river, lake, beach, mountain, and snowflake; the plethora of life forms in the biosphere; the unique branching of every tree; the genetic variation within individual species; and the uniqueness of every human being. Diversity on this scale is consistent with a being who has infinite intelligence, and an ability to simultaneously observe and enjoy this vast diversity.

- The sheer ingenuity and innovation in the design of many aspects of the cosmos, our planet, the nanotechnology of life and many life forms in our biosphere indicate that their maker is highly creative and innovative. Many technological innovations in our modern world were inspired by things observed in nature. Would aeroplanes ever have been invented if birds did not give us the concept of flight? However, this Creator conceived flight in the first place – and many ways to implement it. There are literally millions of innovations throughout the natural world, with many more that we are yet to discover. The Creator is extraordinarily innovative.
- The structure of spiral galaxies, the spectacular colours of a sunset, the play of light through clouds, moonlight on water, the bird chorus in a forest, and the aesthetics of all manner of other aspects of the creation, all suggest that the Creator is an extraordinary artist, who has given humans the ability to appreciate and enjoy these aesthetics.
- His superlative planning and engineering abilities seem to be matched by his care to provide for the necessities of life. Biosphere 2, our best attempt so far to create an artificial self-contained eco-system, demonstrated how difficult this actually is.
- The Creator is not 'in our face' about himself, in that people are free to marvel at the creation, but are not struck by lightning if they don't. The sun shines and the rain falls on the fields of both the good and the bad; weeds, droughts, famines, and economic downturns afflict both alike.
- However, something seems to be wrong. If the Creator possesses all of the above attributes, then why is there pain and suffering in this world? Why especially, do natural

> disasters occur? Why do weeds, thorns, and thistles grow in the gardens of 'good' people just as readily as in the gardens of those who are 'bad'? We don't know what to make of this. Either something has gone wrong, or there is a deeper wisdom at work – or both. Because of the ambiguity, let's put this observation aside for now until we can make more sense of it later in our journey.

Having identified these attributes of the Creator, we now have a benchmark against which we can assess all the religions of the world. No modern religion presents a Creator with such attributes – which is somewhat surprising given the advantage of hindsight. Only three ancient religions do: Judaism, Christianity, and Islam.

The two other major religions of the world, Buddhism and Hinduism, convey no sense of a Creator with the above attributes. Greek and Roman mythology are clearly myths, and the many tribal religious beliefs and practices – which are usually full of myths, superstition, and fear – convey no sense that the creator of the universe has instigated their oral tradition as the primary conduit of his communication with humankind.

So, using creation itself as a benchmark, we have narrowed the candidates down to a shortlist of three. Anyone searching for truth is entitled to ask the same questions of their respective sets of ancient manuscripts: the Jewish scriptures[4] (the Old Testament of the Bible), the Christian scriptures (the New Testament of the Bible), and the Koran.[5] Useful questions to ask are:

---

4. The Jewish scriptures are embraced by Christians as having scriptural authority. However, we will continue to use this term as a synonym for 'The Old Testament'. We will also use the term 'Christian scriptures' as a synonym for the New Testament writings, which are not accepted by Judaism.
5. This spelling (rather than Quran) will be used throughout.

- Does this material contain any prophetic predictions that were clearly fulfilled after the prophecy was written? (A prophecy test.)
- Does this material contain wisdom that is original? Does it carry a sense of its source being 'out of this world' because it contains thoughts and ideas that go beyond the archaeologically-recorded thinking of the culture in which it was written?[6] (Wisdom tests.)
- Does the material convey a sense of the creator of the universe speaking directly to humanity, revealing what he is like, along with his plans and purposes? Does it speak both to individuals and to humankind as a whole? (Communication tests.)

The Koran has borrowed many of its concepts about God from Jewish and Christian sources. This is to be expected given that it was penned last, more than half a millennium after the Christian writings. Respectfully, the Koran has few descriptions about the nature and character of Allah, and the descriptions that are recorded lack breadth and colour, tending instead to be quite detached and repetitive (for example, 'the compassionate and merciful'). Allah seems aloof from the petty details of human lives. Also, the Koran is written almost entirely in the third person; Mohammad interprets things for the reader, which seems to imply that Allah is not directly knowable by ordinary people.

In contrast to this, the Jewish and Christian scriptures claim

---

6. Using the Koran as an example: how much of the material is original, and not copied from Judaism, Christianity or elsewhere? And to what extend does any original content carry a big picture message to humankind in general, such as 'love your enemies'?

the Creator speaks directly to us through the words of the biblical authors. For example, Isaiah 45:12 states, 'It is I who made the earth and created mankind on it. My own hands stretched out the heavens; I marshalled their starry hosts.' Both sets of scriptures are liberally peppered with descriptions of an infinitely knowing, wise, and powerful God – who is from everlasting to everlasting, and full of compassion, mercy, and love (including tough love when required). Both sets also claim that this God wants to work authentically in the hearts and lives of those who look to him with humility and sincerity – which they also claim he is well able to discern. In fact, these statements about the Creator's capabilities and character form the foundational understanding on which everything else is built: the commandments and instructions, wisdom books, prophetic passages, all the historical narratives and associated commentaries, and the letters in the New Testament. Because their communication of God's thinking and character is closely integrated with real-life situations, they give an understanding about God that is full of nuance and colour.

This picture is further enhanced by the involvement of multiple authors, reflecting a God who is willing and able to work through the lives of many diverse people. This phenomenon is not surprising, because an infinite being would need to do this in order to give greater understanding of what he is like. The diversity that we find in the Bible has relevance for the credibility of other paths that are primarily based on the teaching of a single 'prophet' (such as Islam, Buddhism, Mormonism, Confucianism, and many others). To paint a more complete picture of his depth and breadth, an infinite being would require a myriad of separate stories arising from genuine first-hand relationships with many people.

One might wonder at the seeming presumption of men who spoke and wrote as if God was speaking directly through them. However, we should be careful not to project our 21st century mindset onto earlier generations. Moses defined the laws for prophets in the generations that were to follow him:[7] God himself would raise up prophets, put his words in their mouths, and command them what to say. But Moses also stipulated that a 'prophet' who presumed to speak anything in God's name that God had not commanded him to say must be put to death. The Jewish scriptures have many interesting stories of how God authenticated his prophets, and exposed and judged false prophets who spoke from their own presumption. In the New Testament, the apostle Peter wrote from his personal experience of the prophetic gift at work in the Church:

> Above all, you must understand that no prophecy of Scripture came about by the prophet's own interpretation of things. For prophecy never had its origin in the human will, but prophets, though human, spoke from God as they were carried along by the Holy Spirit (2 Peter 1:20-21).

Returning to our main thread, it seems that the ancient writings that best describe the Creator consistently with the ten attributes we have identified, is the combination of ancient Jewish and Christian texts that comprise the modern Bible. Given that Judaism rejects Jesus as Messiah and all Christian writings, we could take a lowest-common-denominator approach, and investigate only the Jewish scriptures. However, Jesus has clearly made an enormous impact on history. The Christian scriptures claim that Jesus fulfilled many prophecies in the Jewish scriptures, and that Jesus modelled what God is like. Some of the New Testament teaching, such as Jesus' Sermon on the Mount, contains extraordinary insight and wisdom.

---

7. Deuteronomy 18:14-22

So, because they are significant, it would be sensible to include the Christian scriptures in our investigation.

The Koran states[8] that Allah (God) inspired both the Torah (Jewish scriptures) and Gospel (Christian scriptures), and it takes some of its teaching from both sources. However, rather than building on them extensively, the Koran goes off on its own, and clearly disagrees with the Jewish and Christian scriptures in a number of important respects. Either the Creator is inconsistent – which is not what we observe from the Creation – or the Koran is not inspired by the same supernatural author behind the Jewish and Christian scriptures. Some readers may wish to flag the Koran, as a place in the road map that they might come back and visit later. For now, we need to be pragmatic and prune our shortlist even further.

For all the reasons we have just explored, the Jewish and Christian writings, as combined together in the modern Bible, seem the most sensible road to take at *spaghetti junction,* to examine the possibility that the creator of the universe has communicated with humankind, and revealed himself and his purposes to us.[9] So, let's take a closer look at the Jewish and Christian scriptures using the modern Bible as a convenient common source for them. We should evaluate the degree to which they are consistent with what

---

8. Surah 3 ayat 2-4: 'He has revealed to you the Book with the Truth, [referring to the Koran] confirming the scriptures which preceded it; for he has already revealed the Torah and the Gospel for the guidance of humankind, and the distinction between right and wrong.' (Trans. NJ Dawood). In Judaism Torah means the books of Moses; however Mohammad seems to have used it generically to mean all the Jewish scriptures. Similarly, he seems to have used the Gospel (singular) generically for all the Christian scriptures.

9. It is extremely practical that such communication should be recorded in written form, as it would become progressively lost and distorted if it was reliant on oral tradition passed down through the generations.

we have observed about the attributes of the Creator that seem self-evident from the creation itself. We should also gain a sense of their contents, and assess the degree to which they are consistent with each other. The name *the Bible* will be used as a generic term that includes both sets of scriptures.

Special Characteristics of the Bible

The Bible contains hundreds of passages portraying the creator of the earth and stars speaking to humankind. For example:

Jewish Scriptures (Old Testament)

> In the beginning, God created the heavens and the earth (Genesis 1:1).
>
> My help comes from the LORD, the Maker of heaven and earth (Psalm 121:2).
>
> Surely the nations are like a drop in a bucket; they are regarded as dust on the scales; he weighs the islands as though they were fine dust (Isaiah 40:15).
>
> It is I who made the earth and created mankind on it. My own hands stretched out the heavens; I marshalled their starry hosts (Isaiah 45:12).
>
> For thus says the Lord, who created the heavens (he is God!), who formed the earth and made it (he established it; he did not create it empty, he formed it to be inhabited!): 'I am the Lord, and there is no other…' (Isaiah 45:18 ESV).

Heaven is my throne, and the earth is my footstool … Has not my hand made all these things, and so they came into being? declares the LORD (Isaiah 66:1-2).

Stand up and praise the LORD your God, who is from everlasting to everlasting … You alone are the LORD. You made the heavens, even the highest heavens, and all their starry host, the earth and all that is on it, the seas and all that is in them. You give life to everything, and the multitudes of heaven worship you (Nehemiah 9:5-6).

He who forms the mountains, who creates the wind, and who *reveals his thoughts to man* … the LORD God Almighty is his name (Amos 4:13, emphasis added).

Do you not know? Have you not heard? The LORD is the everlasting God, the Creator of the ends of the earth. He will not grow tired or weary, and his understanding no one can fathom (Isaiah 40:28).

Christian Scriptures (New Testament)

…from the beginning, when God created the world… (Jesus speaking in Mark 13:19).

Through him all things were made; without him nothing was made that has been made (John 1:3).

There is but one God, the Father, from whom all things came and for whom we live… (1 Corinthians 8:6).

> For in him all things were created: things in heaven and on earth, visible and invisible... (Colossians 1:16).

> ...for you created all things, and by your will they were created and have their being (Revelation 4:11).

> ...him who lives for ever and ever, who created the heavens and all that is in them, the earth and all that is in it... (Revelation 10:6).

> For since the creation of the world God's invisible qualities – his eternal power and divine nature – have been clearly seen, being understood from what has been made... (Romans 1:20).

There are many more excerpts that could be included, but this brief selection should be sufficient for now. Because of these many claims, the Bible can be one of only three things: The truth, a complete fraud, or some garbled and corrupted shambles somewhere on the spectrum between. Let's look at several more characteristics of the Bible, with a view to gaining a sense of whether it is the 'Maker's handbook'.

Many Manuscripts

The biblical text is unlike any other writing from antiquity, in that hundreds of separate early manuscripts have been discovered, along with thousands of portions and fragments of even older manuscripts. Many of these are very old, copied only a century or two after the original. In contrast, the earliest surviving copy of many other ancient manuscripts was made more than a thousand years after the original. While there are minor differences, which you would expect when manuscripts are copied by hand and translated into other languages, all the biblical manuscripts tend to correlate with each other very well. These biblical manuscripts are supported by tens of thousands of other very early manuscripts, both Jewish and Christian, which record sermons and letters quoting the source biblical text. The full text of the Bible could be reconstructed virtually from these alone. The Bible is completely unique in the number and age of ancient supporting manuscripts.

Fulfilled Prophecy

The Bible contains many accurate, fulfilled prophecies. In fact, they are so accurate that in the late 1800s and early 1900s, secular archaeologists and very liberal theologians concluded that they must have been written after the events that they supposedly predicted. However, the discovery of the Dead Sea Scrolls and many other very early manuscripts since then, has shown that it is reasonable to conclude that most of these prophecies were indeed written well before their respective fulfilment.

Biblical prophecy is very different from the obscure ramblings of the likes of Nostradamus. The Old Testament prophets were recognised by their own generation as having been authenticated by God through miraculous signs[1] or supernatural predictive knowledge in everyday events.[2] In the New Testament, the church recognised those in their midst who were empowered by the Holy

1. Moses: The plagues in Egypt (Ex 7 to 12), crossing the sea (Ex 14), manna (Ex 16) and water from the rock (Ex 17), Elijah (1 Kings 17 & 18), and Elisha (2 Kings 2, & 4 to 6)
2. For example, Samuel's reputation, foreknowledge, and predictions to Saul in 1 Samuel 9 & 10.

Spirit with an authentic prophetic gift. Examples include Agabus,[3] several prophets in Antioch,[4] and Philip's four daughters.[5]

Biblical prophecy had two roles. Firstly, God made his thoughts known: he gave guidance and instruction to individuals or the nation as a whole. The second role was predictive: God revealed what he intended to do in the near or distant future. The latter contained multiple detailed specifics, which had an extremely low probability of being fulfilled in the manner described through the normal course of events. When you take even a few of these prophecies together, the probability of them *all* being fulfilled becomes minute – once again, in the order of winning a lottery drawn from all the electrons in the universe. However, taking the Bible as a whole, we are not talking about 'just a few' prophecies…

The Jewish scriptures in particular contain numerous fulfilled prophecies. Many prophecies about the nation of Israel seem to have been spoken and recorded before the events they predicted. Several prophecies that speak of Israel being established again after a very long dispersion were fulfilled with the formation of modern Israel in 1948. There are fulfilled prophecies about the surrounding nations such as Babylon and Tyre. A few, like Daniel 2, accurately predicted the main world governments to the end of this age – and suggest that we may be getting close to 'the time of the end'.

Christian Bible scholars claim that the Jewish scriptures contain more than 300 separate prophecies about the *Messiah*. They say these pointed to and, together, could have been fulfilled only by the historical man, Jesus of Nazareth. These prophecies were obviously written several hundred years earlier. Here are some of them:

---

3. Acts 11:27-28, 21:10-11
4. Acts 13:1-3
5. Acts 21:8-9

- Micah 5:2 states that the Messiah would be born in Bethlehem, and that his origins are from past eternity.
- Malachi 3:1 and Isaiah 40:3 predicted the preparatory ministry of John the Baptist.
- Isaiah 9:1-2 predicted that much of Jesus' time would be spent in Galilee.
- Isaiah 61:1-2 described the work that Jesus would do during his public ministry.
- Psalm 22 accurately described crucifixion, including the dehydration of the victim, 500 years before this style of execution was even invented. It also states that they would cast lots for his clothing.
- Isaiah 52:13-53:12 speaks of a *suffering servant* who would 'pour out his life unto death' and, by doing so, would make a way for many people to receive forgiveness from God and be reconciled to him – not only from Israel, but from many nations.
- Psalm 16:10 predicted Jesus' resurrection; God would not allow his holy one to decay in the grave.
- Daniel 9:26 gave the ballpark date that the Messiah would appear in history, stated that he would be killed,[6] and pre-

---

6. Daniel 9:25-26. This text was written in Babylon, while the Jewish nation was in exile there. 'Know and understand this: From the time the word goes out to restore and rebuild Jerusalem until the Anointed One, the ruler, comes, there will be seven "sevens," and sixty-two "sevens." It will be rebuilt with streets and a trench, but in times of trouble. After the sixty-two "sevens," the Anointed One will be put to death and will have nothing. The people of the ruler who will come will

dicted the destruction of Jerusalem and the temple which followed.

We detour briefly to gain a greater feel for the calibre of biblical prophecy. Psalm 22 begins with the words, 'My God, my God, why have you forsaken me?' On the cross, shortly before he died, Jesus recited these words in a loud cry. He was clearly pointing to this prophetic psalm, which includes the sentence 'They have pierced my hands and feet,' and a lot of other specific descriptions, including 'They … cast lots for my clothing.' It was fulfilled in astonishing detail that day. Jewish scholars struggle to understand the suffering servant of Isaiah 52:13 to 53:12. They usually interpret this prophecy as speaking of a completely separate person from the Messiah. However, Daniel 9:26 strongly suggests that they are one and the same. More than this, Daniel speaks of a landmark moment 483 years after 'the decree to restore and rebuild Jerusalem' (v. 25) – a predicted timeframe that came to historical fruition within the years of Jesus' public life and death. Then, exactly as Daniel had predicted, the city and temple were destroyed a few years later, within that same generation. Daniel uses the term the *Anointed One*, the *ruler* (in 9:25), which clearly refers to the Messiah. There is only one Jewish man of historical significance who came in that narrow window of time before the city and temple were destroyed, who was 'cut off and had nothing.' He was Jesus of Nazareth.

In the Christian scriptures (NT), Jesus regularly explained to his disciples that they were seeing prophecies from the Jewish scriptures being fulfilled before their eyes. Their own knowledge of the scriptures no doubt enabled them to recognise some of these

---

destroy the city and the sanctuary. The end will come like a flood: War will continue until the end, and desolations have been decreed.' (Note: A 'seven' means seven years.)

prophetic passages without the need for explanation. But in a number of places, the gospels record that the disciples only realised later that other prophetic scriptures had been fulfilled while Jesus was with them. The sheer volume of prophetic fulfilment in the New Testament gospel narratives makes them very special.

However, with the New Testament itself, our prophecy test is not so clear cut, because Jesus' predictions of his own death and resurrection were fulfilled well before they were written down in the gospels.[7] In Acts 11:28 Luke records that the Holy Spirit enabled Agabus to predict a severe famine would spread over the entire Roman world. Luke adds the comment that this prophecy was fulfilled during the reign of Claudius, implying that he wrote Acts after this time. Those who have had the privilege of seeing God do something very special – such as a miraculous healing – feel they would not dare embellish the details of what actually occurred. They can project this onto those who were close to Jesus and who saw everything he did while he was among them, and can easily trust the integrity of the biblical writers. However, many readers will not have first-hand experiences they can leverage like this.

All the narrative passages in the Old and New Testaments are quite matter-of-fact in the style they use to narrate miraculous events. Nevertheless, in pursuing our road map, we are looking for more objective evidence than this. Consider that when the three synoptic gospels of Matthew, Mark, and Luke were written, many people who had witnessed those events were still alive, and these witnesses would have raised an outcry against the authors if the incidents and aspects of Jesus' life and ministry had been fabricated or embellished. If any fabrication had occurred there would have been hints of this in the material written by others as the church grew.

---

7. The gospels were written one or two decades later, and perhaps fifty or sixty years later for John's Gospel.

So, we can attribute a measure of trustworthiness to the earlier gospels especially for this reason alone. Luke is highly regarded as a historian by even secular scholars who specialise in the first century, because he often provides background comments and ancillary details in the events he records. His reliable correlation with other historical records in those ancillary details suggests that he was also reliable in the main details of his narrative.

The New Testament contains much prophetic material which speaks about events that are yet future in the build-up to Jesus' return. Although these prophecies state there will come a day when they will all be fulfilled and can be viewed with hindsight, that day has obviously not yet arrived.

However, one lengthy passage of Jesus' teaching was prophetic, and spoke of things that were to come after he had left his disciples. This passage is recorded in three of the gospels[8] and most scholars agree they were all written before the events Jesus predicted. Because this discussion took place on the Mount of Olives just outside of Jerusalem it is often referred to as the Olivet Discourse. In this teaching, Jesus predicted the destruction of the temple, and went on to describe what his followers should expect to occur in their immediate generation, in subsequent generations, and in the final build-up to his return. The temple – as well as the whole city – was destroyed by the Roman army in AD 70; quite literally not one stone was left upon another, as Jesus predicted. A number of other things that Jesus predicted in these passages have also been fulfilled over the many generations since.

So, we find some amazing fulfilled prophecies in both the Jewish and Christian scriptures. No other documents on the planet come anywhere near them in this regard. The God of the Bible even

---

8. Matthew 24, Mark 13, and Luke 21.

claims that his ability to accurately foretell the future is proof of his authenticity.[9] Biblical prophecy is truly astonishing and completely unique in its breadth, detail, and accuracy. It seems to be a deliberate and compelling signpost, pointing us to the reality that the human writers had outside help.

Historical Narrative and Archaeology

Archaeological digs, when interpreted with academic integrity, confirm the accuracy of the geographical and historical context of many biblical passages. Several digs, for example at Jericho, even confirm some of the specific details of the narrative. It is therefore not unreasonable to extrapolate this accuracy to the rest of the associated narrative which describes God at work.

Confirmations are not confined to archaeological sites in Palestine, wider Mesopotamia, North Africa and the ancient Roman world. Some ideographs used in ancient Chinese *oracle bone carvings*[10] have a surprisingly close correlation with events recorded in Genesis, the first book of the Bible.[11] Modern astronomical software – which can be run on a notebook or PC – can wind back the moon and planets to any date in the past, revealing several intriguing astronomical events. For example, on the Jewish Passover in AD 33 (a commonly accepted date for when Jesus was crucified), the moon rose over the evening horizon in full eclipse and coloured blood red. The eclipse started at three o'clock in the afternoon while the moon was still below the horizon in Jerusalem. This was the hour that Jesus died. Now, eclipses are more frequent

---

9. Isaiah 44:6-8, 44:25-26.
10. From the time of the Shang Dynasty, 1750-1050 BC.
11. Nelson, E. R. & Broadberry, R. E. (1994). *Genesis and the mystery Confucius couldn't solve*. St. Louis, MS: Concordia Publishing.

close to the equinoxes, but what is the mathematical chance of that precise timing merely being a coincidence?[12]

Wisdom that is Out of this World

While many wise sayings for harmonious living can be found in ancient writings, like those of Confucius, or modern ones like those of Gandhi, these tend to be more akin to modern humanism. By contrast, biblical wisdom is tightly integrated with the sense that our lives are in full view of the creator God, and that harmonious living should be an extension of harmony *with him*.

The laws of Moses contained in the Jewish scriptures are holistic and wise, and lay a tremendous foundation for a fair and just society. The Ten Commandments were just the beginning. Moses established a workable, fair, and just system for handling disputes. Other laws established *cities of refuge*, where a person accused of killing someone could flee, and would be safe until they received a fair trial. There were provisions for the poor, and laws for citizens who got themselves into debt. There were even instructions for the fair and generous treatment of foreigners. The dietary laws make surprisingly good sense when understood from the perspective of modern medicine.

Some of Jesus' teaching in the Sermon on the Mount was radically different from normal human thinking, and especially the thinking of his day. Therefore, the disciples of Jesus did not understand many of his teachings or decisions until they had the benefit of hindsight several years later. It is remarkable that Jesus taught all

---

12. See www.bethlehemstar.com/the-day-of-the-cross/the-celestial-dirge/. Other pages on this site also make interesting reading, including its claim about the *Star of Bethlehem* that caused astronomers from the East to search for a very special Jewish king who had been born.

this as a young man in his early thirties, rather than as an elderly sage who could draw from a lifetime of experience.[13] The just and holistic nature of the Mosaic Law was profoundly different from the practices of the surrounding nations of that time, where 'might has right' was the basic law of the day. The Christian concepts of *servant leadership*, *love your enemies*, and *while we were yet sinners Christ died for us* were counter-cultural in their day. They remain so today in societies that are largely untouched by Christianity. The Jewish and Christian scriptures were so radically different from the 'wisdom' in the surrounding cultures, they both seem to have come from a source that is out of this world.

---

13. Some of Jesus' abilities were remarkable for a man his age. He could always respond superbly in the flat-footed heat of the moment. For example, Jesus deftly outmanoeuvred the malevolent cunning and teamwork of the sharpest and most educated men in the nation who were twice his age. They had schemed together and devised a clever way to trap him, baiting it with seemingly sincere flattery to put him off-guard. See Luke 20:20-26.

Major Bible Themes:

Foundations

The biblical text contains several major themes, and numerous minor ones. In it the God of the Bible – who I will refer to as simply God for the sake of brevity in the following sections – reveals what he is like. It documents some of the things he did in earlier human history. It spells out the big picture, and gives a road map for humankind as a whole. However, God obviously also intended it should be read and digested as part of the devotional life of individuals who seek to know him better and live according to his plans and purposes. It is also full of many themes that span the spectrum of human existence and experience, and spells out many aspects of godly character, loving relationships, and wholesome living.

The Bible also gives a very plausible explanation as to why there is pain and suffering in this world – natural disasters, weeds in our gardens, and why we all age and eventually die. What it claims Jesus accomplished through his life, death, and resurrection is very tightly integrated with these realities.

The following sections give an overview of the Bible's contents and major themes. A number of scripture references are provided for further research through the use of a printed Bible, and/or a free on-line Bible via a Google search of individual references.

The Creator's Identity

The very first sentence of the Jewish scriptures says, 'In the beginning God created the heavens and the earth.'[1] The Hebrew word for God is *ĕ·lō·hîm*, which is plural. Genesis 1:26 reads, 'Then God said, 'Let us make man in our image, in our likeness, and let them rule … over all the earth…' Once again, the Hebrew wording is plural. This is not like the 'royal we' the Queen uses. The wording conveys a genuine plural meaning. So, the Jewish scriptures state that God is not a single infinite being, but a plurality.

- Genesis 1:2 says, 'and the Spirit of God was hovering over the waters.' The term *Spirit of God* occurs on thirteen other occasions in the OT. A similar term, *the Spirit of the Lord*, occurs twenty-six times. God also uses the term *my Spirit* fourteen times when speaking to or through one of the prophets. These all speak of situations where people were supernaturally empowered to fulfil God's purposes. It is possible to understand this as God speaking about himself, in the same way as we might say 'my spirit was crushed'. However, it is also possible to interpret this as speaking about a separate divine entity who had a specific role of empowering people.
- Isaiah 9:6 says, 'For to us a child is born, to us a son is given, and the government will be on his shoulders. And he will be called Wonderful Counsellor, Mighty God, Everlasting Father, Prince of Peace.' This is a prophecy about the Messiah. It says that he will be a human child, but also Mighty God. Once again it is possible to interpret

---

1. Genesis 1:1

this as referring to this child being one and the same as the Everlasting Father. However, coming to Earth and being born as a human child suggests a separate divine entity.

The Christian scriptures clarify things further, and say that God is three separate infinite entities or personalities: The Father, the Word (Jesus), and the Holy Spirit. They worked together to create the universe and biosphere. The New Testament indicates that they enjoy perfect harmony and communication, at an infinite level, in complete unity. It says that they are not identical, that each is different and has played a unique and mutually dependent role in their relationship together, and in human history. These separate roles are still at work today and will continue throughout eternity. However, when one does anything, he is articulating or enacting the collective will of all three. Their harmony and unity is such that they are effectively one.

- While they all were involved in the planning of cosmic history, it would seem that the Father is somehow the master planner, and is the one that we tend to think of when we refer to God in the singular. This is partly because God the Father was the one who revealed himself in the Old Testament record which can be viewed as 'the Age of the Father'.
- Jesus' role is being the 'Word of God'.[2] The New Testament says he was the one who articulated their collective will, and spoke the cosmos into being.[3]
  - Jesus has the role of appearing in human form. The clearest example was as the man Jesus. However, there

2. John 1
3. Psalm 33:6, John 1:3, Colossians 1:15-17, and Hebrews 1:2

were several events in the Old Testament where God appeared briefly in human form. The first was walking in the Garden of Eden and talking directly with Adam and Eve.[4] Another was together with two angels, to speak with Abraham and tell him that he, an old man, and his wife Sarah, who was long past menopause, were going to be miraculously enabled to have a son through whom the nation of Israel came into existence. At that time, he also told Abraham what he was about to do to Sodom and Gomorrah.[5] God often appeared in human form speaking with Moses.[6] It is unclear whether it was the Father, or the Word who appeared in these cases, but it could have been the latter. He may have been the fourth man that Nebuchadnezzar saw in the furnace – one that 'looked like a son of God' – although that could have been an angel.[7]

- While all three love us sufficiently to undergo what was required to restore life and relationship after *sin* had done its damage, Jesus was the most appropriate one to do this.
- The Bible uses many names for Jesus, which reflect various roles he has played. As mentioned, one of these is as the Word of God. The name Jesus means *saviour*. Isaiah lists several which show that Jesus was, and is, an integral part of God.[8] Because of his special and unique

---

4. Genesis 3:8-19
5. Genesis 18
6. Numbers 12:8
7. Daniel 3
8. 'For unto us a child is born … And he will be called … Mighty God, Everlasting Father, Prince of Peace' (Isaiah 9:6-7).

conception,[9] he was called the Son of God during his time on Earth.[10] While he acknowledged this term was appropriate,[11] he preferred to refer to himself as the *son of man* when he spoke in public. This was much easier for people on the edges to accept, but it also had a cryptic meaning. God sometimes used this term when speaking to various prophets – for example, Ezekiel – and, more importantly, it also had a special messianic significance.[12]

– While the Son appeared in human form as Jesus, the New Testament says that his 'Age' in human history is yet to come – his messianic rule of the earth as 'King of Kings and Lord of Lords.'[13] In eternity, his role will be fully integrated with the other two members of the Trinity.[14]

---

9. '"How will this be," Mary asked the angel, "since I am a virgin?" The angel answered, "The Holy Spirit will come on you, and the power of the Most High will overshadow you. So the holy one to be born will be called the Son of God."'(Luke 1:34-35).
10. By John the Baptist: 'I have seen and I testify that this is the Son of God' (John 1:34).
11. He did so when charged under oath by the high priest at his trial before the religious leaders. (Matthew 26:63-66).
12. 'In my vision at night I looked, and there before me was one like a *son of man*, coming with the clouds of heaven. He approached the Ancient of Days and was led into his presence. He was given authority, glory and sovereign power; all nations and peoples of every language worshiped him. His dominion is an everlasting dominion that will not pass away, and his kingdom is one that will never be destroyed' (Daniel 7:13-14, emphasis added).
13. Revelation 19:11-16
14. He is 'the Alpha and Omega, the First and the Last, the Beginning and the End' (Revelation 22:13).

- The Holy Spirit's role is to influence and empower men and women to understand and glorify God and Jesus, and to fulfil God's plans and purposes through them. The New Testament says that the Holy Spirit was referred to as the Spirit of God, and the Spirit of the Lord in the Old Testament. He revealed things to various prophets, and empowered other men and women of God to perform extraordinary feats. However, because of the role he has played in it, the last 2,000 years – the age of the Church – is, in a sense, the age of the Holy Spirit. In fact, Jesus said that he had to depart temporarily to better facilitate this age.[15]

The identity of the Messiah is the main point of departure between Judaism and Christianity. Judaism rejects Jesus of Nazareth and the claims about him in the Christian scriptures. Jews are still waiting for the Messiah to come. Christians obviously have a very different view on who Jesus was, and are longing for his return. We will explore this crucial issue further in the section on Jesus in History.

The Nature and Character of God

A significant theme throughout the Bible is God's revelation of himself. The earlier section, Which Way Is Up, identified ten objective attributes of the creator of the universe and biosphere. The God of the Bible claims to have those same attributes. However, the Jewish and Christian scriptures provide information about the Creator that is not readily apparent from the creation itself, such as: his character, attitudes, thinking, and purposes; and that he is a plurality.

---

15. John 15:26 and 16:7-15.

- Throughout the Bible, God consistently defines himself as an infinitely knowing, wise, and powerful being, who is from eternity past[16] and 'from everlasting to everlasting.'[17]
- The Bible says that God sees and understands the phenomenally complex interplay of minute details of people's lives down through the generations, to the extent that several passages claim that he foreknew each one of us from the foundation of time.[18,19]
- The Bible claims that God can foresee what will occur in situations many years, and even generations, into the future, and the accumulated influences that will shape and define what we will think, say and do. This is not saying that we are all robots. It is just that he understands us incredibly well – infinitely in fact. It is worth exploring this a bit further.

---

16. 'Your throne was established long ago; you are from all eternity' (Psalm 93:2).
17. 1 Chronicles 16:36; 29:10; Nehemiah 9:5
18. 'All the days ordained for me were written in your book before one of them came to be' (Psalm 139:16). 'For he chose us in him before the creation of the world' (Ephesians 1:4). 'calling forth the generations from the beginning' (Isaiah 41:4).
19. This implies he foreknew all the chance events and delicate moments that brought about all the marriages (and other unions) in each family tree, all the way back to Adam and Eve. More than that, it implies that he foreknew the individual sperm in each conception in the hereditary sequence that delivered to each one of us our unique DNA – for everyone on the planet. This is a huge claim, which is unthinkable from a secular perspective. However, when one reflects on this, we can see how this is perfectly reasonable and what we should expect from a being who is genuinely *infinite*, who sees and thoroughly understands the complex interplay between myriads of minute details within his creation, and their compounding effects over time.

While he understands us infinitely, he also loves us infinitely. As loving parents, we enjoy and cultivate our own children's individuality and ability to make their own decisions. Even from a young age we encourage them to paint their own pictures and engage in free play. While we understand them well enough to second-guess many of their decisions, they are the ones who make them. We try to instil good judgement so that in due course they will be equipped to make big decisions of their own. In the same way, our loving heavenly Father delights in our own unique individuality, and has created an environment where we can grow in our ability to consistently make good choices and carry responsibility well. These are intrinsic components of good character. In many ways, what distinguishes a good decision is defined by the risks and potential to make a bad decision. As we make the transition from children to adults, and mature further in this life, God gives us big choices of our own to make. These include whether we even want to have a relationship with him. While he understands us so well that he can do more than merely second-guess our thoughts and decisions, these are nevertheless our decisions to make. The Bible repeatedly says that we are responsible for the good and bad choices that we exercise over the course of our lifetime.

- The Bible claims that God's infinite understanding gives him the perspective and good judgement to always say and do what will prove to be right in the long term.[20]
- The Bible says that God is infinitely holy. This is not an everyday term in 21st century society. Merriam-Webster

---

20. 'righteousness and justice are the foundation of his throne' (Psalm 97:2).

defines *holy* as meaning 'exalted or worthy of complete devotion as one perfect in goodness and righteousness.' The Bible gives us glimpses of heavenly worship where awareness of God's holiness is a central theme.[21]

- The Bible describes God's character as being deeply loving and merciful.[22,23] However, this is a very intelligent love. The scriptures recount many incidents in which God used 'tough love' to confront individuals and nations, thereby bringing them around to a better understanding and way of living. It also says that God is prepared to orchestrate large scale lethal or devastating judgement to rein in pride and evil when other options have been exhausted.[24]

- The Bible indicates that God desires harmonious and high-integrity relationships with all his creation. It claims that this is an attribute of the Trinity itself,[25] and is therefore a foundational characteristic of who God is. The biblical record demonstrates this in his relationship with Adam and Eve before the fall; with Enoch, Noah, Abraham, David, and many other individuals; but most of all in the relationship between the Father and Jesus during his time on Earth.

---

21. Isaiah 6; Revelation 4.
22. 'The Lord is compassionate and gracious, slow to anger, abounding in love' (Psalm 103:8).
23. 'He will judge the world in righteousness, and the peoples with equity.' (Psalm 98:9).
24. For example, the Flood (Genesis 6:5-13), Sodom and Gomorrah (Genesis 18:20; 19:1-29), judgements against the nation of Israel on several occasions, and the apocalyptic judgements at the end of this age (Book of Revelation).
25. 'Whoever does not love does not know God, because God is love' (1 John 4: 8).

It also shows that God wanted a direct relationship with the nation of Israel, and later the church as collective entities. Therefore, it is not difficult to understand that God wants us to enjoy harmonious relationships with him and with each other. Various prophetic passages declare that perfect harmony will characterise both the final millennium of finite human history and the mainstream of future eternity.

- The Bible declares that God deeply loves every human and desires the very best for each of us. Further, it says God is just and that everyone will eventually reap what they have sown in their life. Those of us who are conscientious parents gain some insight into God's benevolent heart for his children. From times when we needed to make a hard call against one of our own children because they were wilfully self-centred and inconsiderate towards others, we also gain some insights into God's heart towards wickedness on the earth. The Bible says that, while he may ultimately be compelled to do so, God gains no pleasure from moving against people in judgement.[26]

In the opening section (Telling Truth from Fiction), we observed that truth is bigger than any one of us. This obviously also applies to our understanding of God himself. In Isaiah 55:8-9, God says,

> For my thoughts are not your thoughts. Neither are your ways my ways … As the heavens are higher than the earth, so are my ways higher than your ways and my thoughts than your thoughts.

---

26. 'For I take no pleasure in the death of anyone, declares the Lord. Repent and live' (Ezekiel 18:32).

As one walks the journey of faith with God, one becomes increasingly aware of this reality. But this is what we should expect in a relationship with an infinite being. It applies to every aspect of our thinking and life experience. Even after exchanging fiction for God's truth in some major aspect of our perception, we later find there are many nuances and new depths to which that truth can be taken. Of course, God also foresees the significance of events that are yet future, which we will only understand later with hindsight.

The Bible says that God is very willing to reveal himself, his thoughts and his ways as appropriate, to those who are genuinely humble. Such people are willing to recalibrate themselves according to what they learn, and are eager for the gentle working of God to gradually transform them, deep in their being, to be more like him in nature and character. The Bible states that God desires first-hand relationships of this calibre with every one of us. As mentioned in the previous section, Jesus taught that loving relationships characterise the Trinity itself. They are also an outworking of God's nature and character in us, being a reflection of God himself who made humankind in his own image.[27]

The Spiritual World that Surrounds Us

Having experienced only the material world, it is impossible for us to understand much about spiritual realms. The Bible gives us insight into how spiritual dynamics touched the generations described in various narrative passages. It says these timeless insights are applicable and relevant to all generations, including our own. The spiritual conflict that touches individuals, families, societies, and nations seems to involve moral power plays, significant choices, and

---

27. 'So God created mankind in his own image, in the image of God he created them; male and female he created them' (Genesis 1:27).

influences that affect future choices. These dynamics also involve who or what we worship, loyalties and allegiances, and the ongoing conflict between lies and truth. These accumulate into spiritual darkness or light, depending on which spiritual seeds have been sown. It also says that the spiritual climate in which children are raised will deeply influence their lives, and the lives of their own children and grandchildren.

The Bible also gives a number of significant glimpses into the spiritual realm, and hints that there are at least hundreds of millions of angels.[28] It indicates there are different sorts of angels. Some are very powerful spiritual beings, with the ability to perceive and understand many events and situations simultaneously. Others are more 'ordinary'. They are all in perfect harmony with God's plans and purposes. Matthew 22:30 suggests that, unlike humans, angels do not have the ability to procreate, but they are perfectly content to play the roles God has assigned to them.

However, the Bible includes several statements about Satan and demons, who are angels that have rebelled against God and have since hardened themselves completely beyond recovery. The Bible strongly warns against them, and describes their implacable enmity towards God, their agenda to oppose and destroy at every opportunity, and their malevolent and deadly power plays for the hearts and minds of men, women, and children. It describes how worshipping anyone or anything other than God, and our buying into the clever, sugar-coated lies and deception from the demonic realm, gives them strong spiritual footholds that continue to blind us to the real truth about God. Further, the Bible warns that the demonic

---

28. 'Then I looked and heard the voice of many angels, numbering thousands upon thousands, and ten thousand times ten thousand. They encircled the throne and the living creatures and the elders' (Revelation 5:11).

realm feeds us twisted thinking and views of the world that justify and make admirable words, actions, and lifestyles that are far away from how God designed us to live.

The Bible does not say how many angels fell, although it probably was a minority. However, vandalism is much easier than building and restoring, and over the generations the demonic forces have been very effective at cultivating and exploiting human weaknesses, and injecting lies and twisted thinking into the norms and mindsets of whole nations, societies, and subcultures. One might ask the question: Why would God let these dark forces range free, creating such mayhem and misery among humankind? However, the Bible says they do *not* have free rein, but are subject to boundaries that God sets, and that he and the angels work tirelessly to restrict demonic ploys, malice and vandalism, and to repair and restore people and situations. But we need to understand more about 'the big picture' before we can understand God's perspective and purpose in not sidelining the demonic realm immediately after their rebellion – and for creating them in the first place, given that he foreknew the havoc they would cause. So, we will revisit this at several points over the remaining sections.

It is worth noting that the lies we fall for most easily are those we want to be true, because they stroke our ego, fulfil a fantasy, or pander to our pride. What the Bible calls sin is relevant here. We want our self-centred thinking and actions to be OK, and God's perspective on the consequences to be mistaken. The Bible says that, from the beginning of humankind, the satanic forces have been misrepresenting God. They twist, undermine, and deny what God has revealed as truth, even making false accusations against God's character. Being aware of spiritual realities can help us to discern truth from fiction. However, while these sorts of lies should be fairly easy to recognise, the web of clever half-truths that come with them can make things quite murky, and discernment becomes difficult. Lies from the demonic realm have a spiritual power that can tie us up in knots, preventing us from seeing the truth.

The spiritual world has far more influence on humanity than most people realise. In the story of the nation of Israel, idolatry opened the way for all manner of violence and wickedness – by kings, nobles, and the ordinary populace alike. The New Testament mentions a number of people who unwittingly became pawns in satanic attacks on Jesus and later the church. The Bible also identifies sinful living as being a vicious cycle that locks people into spiritual blindness, unhealthy thinking, and attitudes that prevent them from turning to God.[29]

God's identity, nature, and character are foundational themes that are re-emphasised throughout the Jewish and Christian scriptures. Much of the prophetic content found there is framed by an acknowledgement of God's unchanging nature and character. The Bible commends men and women who embrace this understanding, and live by it. A good understanding of who God is, and what he is like, helped lift the heroes of the Bible above self-serving agendas and ambitions, into ways of thinking and living that were motivated by a genuine desire to please God. It can do the same for us.

---

29. Jeremiah 16:12, John 3:19

Major Bible Themes:

History from God's Perspective

A sizeable proportion of the Bible is narrative. The narratives describe God's sovereign activity in relation to the conditions, events, actions, and lives of individuals and nations. Surprisingly, many narrative passages are characterised by warts-and-all honesty. They often include what God said through a prophet to individuals or to the nation, to communicate his perspective on the situation they faced. These accounts contribute considerable nuance and colour to our understanding of God himself. The narrative passages, together with the prophetic books and letters, give a good sense of God's perspective on human history, and his plans and purposes with respect to the big picture.

Main Historical Periods and Events

The Bible provides a historical narrative demonstrating God's involvement and influence on human history over many generations – with the nations and humankind in general, the nation of Israel, the life and ministry of Jesus, and the early years of the church.

The main epochs and watershed events that the Bible records are:

Jewish Scriptures (Old Testament)

- The creation

- The fall
- Growth of population and wickedness
- The flood
- Babel and the origin of separate languages
- The call of Abraham, and the origin of Israelite and Arab nations
- Captivity of the Israelites in Egypt
- The Exodus and foundations for the nation of Israel (with many applications for humane societies in general)
- Conquering the land: the time before the kings
- The first three kings: Saul, David and Solomon (David's son)
- Idolatry, division of the nation and life under their subsequent kings
- Exile of the Jewish nation to Babylon, and significant events there
- Return of a remnant to the homeland

Christian Scriptures (New Testament)

- Jesus' life on Earth
- Birth and growth of the early church

The prophetic and wisdom books of the Old Testament and the letters in the New Testament are all anchored in history. The narrative passages record historical information, and provide context to enable us to understand the other books more easily. These in turn feed considerable extra detail and colour back into our understanding of the narrative passages themselves. Much could be said about each of the above bullet points. However, the purpose of this section is to give a brief overview that conveys a sense of the Bible's narrative passages.

Jesus in History

The New Testament documents Jesus – what he did and said. It also makes many claims about who he was and is, the central role he plays in human history, and the role he will continue to play in the future big picture of cosmic history.

Many prophecies in the Old Testament pointed to Jesus' coming, and described in advance many aspects of his life and death. They predicted:

- the location and general timing of his birth (Micah 5:2-5a; Daniel 9:24-26).
- the radically different nature of his ministry, both in its style and supernatural dimension (Isaiah 61:1-2).[1]
- the horrific nature of his death, and what he accomplished spiritually through it (Isaiah 52:13 to 53:12 and Psalm 22).
- how his life, death, and resurrection introduced a new spiritual dynamic into humankind, evidenced in the growth of the early church. And the results can still be seen in most parts of the worldwide church today. Paul described this

---

1. Jesus read this prophecy in the synagogue in Nazareth and appropriated this as speaking about him. He was nearly killed by the townspeople as a consequence (Luke 4:14-30).

quite comprehensively in Romans 8, from his perspective of first-hand experience and hindsight.

The New Testament gospels – which means good news – give us historical accounts of Jesus' life, teaching, and miraculous demonstrations of God's endorsement, including many healings and exorcisms.[2] They reveal God's desire to break through into the hearts and lives of ordinary people. The gospels make statements about Jesus such as:

- 'This is my son, whom I love … Listen to him.'[3]
- 'For God did not send his Son into the world to condemn the world, but to save the world through him.'[4]

The book of Acts gives an account of the growth of the early church, and some of the key events involving the church in Jerusalem and Samaria, and its later expansion into the then-known world through the travels of Paul and others. It contains several statements about Jesus such as, 'Salvation is found in no one else, for there is no other name under heaven given to mankind by which we must be saved.'[5]

---

2. The healings and exorcisms were also performed through Jesus closest twelve disciples – also through another group of seventy-two others. (Luke 10:1-23)
3. God himself speaking in an audible voice at Jesus' baptism, and later to the three disciples who accompanied him on the mountain where he was supernaturally encouraged and strengthened for the ordeal ahead. (Matthew 3:17, Mark 9:7, and Luke 9:35)
4. John 3:17
5. Peter courageously speaking about Jesus to the religious leaders who had instigated Jesus' crucifixion (Acts 4:12).

The letters of Paul and various apostles tease out detailed understanding about Jesus, of what God achieved through his life, death, and resurrection; and how this event broke the power of the demonic realm, so it could no longer hold us in the darkness of its malicious lies. The letters also describe in detail how this newly released spiritual dynamic impacts our lives as Christians. For example,

> The Son is the image of the invisible God, the firstborn over all creation. For in him all things were created: things in heaven and on earth, visible and invisible, whether thrones or powers or rulers or authorities; all things have been created through him and for him. He is before all things, and in him all things hold together. And he is the head of the body, the church; he is the beginning and the firstborn from among the dead, so that in everything he might have the supremacy. For God was pleased to have all his fullness dwell in him, and through him to reconcile to himself all things, whether things on earth or things in heaven, by making peace through his blood, shed on the cross. Once you were alienated from God and were enemies in your minds because of your evil behaviour. But now he has reconciled you by Christ's physical body through death to present you holy in his sight, without blemish and free from accusation – if you continue in your faith, established and firm, and do not move from the hope held out in the gospel (Colossians 1:15-23).

During the time of his ministry Jesus said some very significant things about himself. These statements caused the religious leaders of his day to choke, because they were so preposterous for an ordinary human to claim. Either they were the ravings of an egocentric madman, or they were the real and remarkable truth. Things Jesus said about himself included:

- When Jesus was on trial before the Jewish Sanhedrin, Israel's national leadership, he was charged under oath before God to tell them whether he was the Messiah, the Son of God. He was fully aware of the significance of the question – and that he was effectively signing his own death warrant, because it was serious blasphemy for a mere human to claim this for himself, and he knew they would not believe him. Yet, under oath, Jesus told them very plainly that he was and, more than that, in the future they would see him fulfil the significant messianic prophecy of Daniel 7:13-14.[6]
- 'I am the way and the truth and the life. No one comes to the Father except through me.' (John 14:6)[7]
- 'When you have lifted up the Son of Man [predicting his crucifixion], then you will know that I am he and that I do nothing on my own but speak just what the Father has taught me' (John 8:28).
- 'I am telling you what I have seen in the Father's presence…' (John 8:38).
- 'I have not come on my own; God sent me' (John 8:42).
- 'Very truly I tell you, before Abraham was born, I am!' (John 8:58).[8]

---

6. Matthew 26:64; Mark 14:62.
7. Many dismiss this statement as being extremely arrogant. Yet it seems that Jesus said it because it was the plain truth, and his listeners – and we today – needed to hear it.
8. The 'I am' was a shortened form of God's name which was revealed to Moses. Literally translated it means 'I am who I am – from infinity past to infinity future.' So Jesus said that he pre-existed Abraham and was in fact God.

- In a private discussion with his disciples he predicted what would happen to the church through the centuries to the end of the age, which would be marked by his return to earth in great power and authority.[9]

Some of these points convey the prophetic context and purpose of Jesus' death. However, the horrific brutality of the events of that day, and the pure hatred towards Jesus, far exceeded what one might have expected from reading those prophecies. Later, Jesus' disciples remembered what he told them, and what they observed about his demeanour, during the build-up to the crucifixion. After the crucifixion and resurrection, they finally had the perspective to understand what they had heard and seen. Clearly, Jesus had been fully aware of what was coming. John records what Jesus told the crowd on one occasion in that final week.[10] This passage gives good insight into Jesus' foreknowledge of what was about to occur, and what he was thinking as he steeled himself for what he knew was only days away. Luke records that Jesus courageously 'set his face' to go to Jerusalem.[11] It is Luke's alertness as a doctor that also saw fit to record that, in Gethsemane, Jesus' state of awareness in prayer was so intense he was sweating, even though the nights at that time of year were cold – and that his sweat had some blood mixed in it.[12] Jesus knew the immensity of the moment, discerned the dark spiritual forces that were malevolently arrayed against him, and understood that what he needed to do was going to be the

---

9. Matthew 24; Mark 13; and Luke 21.
10. John 12:20-26
11. Luke 9:51
12. Modern medical literature documents this as a rare condition called *haematidrosis*, which is usually a symptom of acute fear and extreme stress. Luke 22:44.

spiritual game-changer, not just for humankind, but for eternity. In complete awareness of what would unfold, he valiantly chose to wait there in the moonlight for his betrayer, Judas – a close friend for more than three years – to arrive, leading the temple guard to arrest him, and start the avalanche of the next sixteen hours.

Christianity is a very curious movement, in that it celebrates the excruciating and ignominious execution of its leader, and calls that day Good Friday. However, as we gradually grasp church history, and the even bigger prophetic picture, we begin to realise that this was not the end; it genuinely was just the beginning.

Few people doubt the historicity of Jesus' life and death. Even hostile witnesses such as the Roman historian Tacitus confirm it. However, we need to seriously consider and assess the truth of the claim that God raised Jesus from the dead on the Sunday morning that immediately followed. If this is not true, and the bones of Jesus are still somewhere in or near Jerusalem – which is the view of most secular scholars and some very liberal theologians – then Jesus did not fulfil the key prophetic passages and therefore cannot be the Messiah. His death would not be the spiritual watershed in human history that the New Testament claims it to be. Furthermore, the growth of the early church and the church down through the generations since then would have been founded on a monstrous myth and delusion. Many books have been written on this subject and we cannot really do it justice here.[13] There are also a number of web pages that present careful arguments and lists of evidence that support the resurrection as being a true event – and some sites that argue against this. However, here are some key things for us to consider:

---

13. Three popular books for the pro position are *Who Moved the Stone* by Frank Morison, *Evidence That Demands a Verdict* by Josh McDowell, and *The Case for Christ* by Lee Strobel.

- No formal Roman or Jewish historical documents have been uncovered that independently verify the resurrection claim. While this might be disappointing, it is what we should reasonably expect. The Jewish leadership was hardly likely to document support for a claim they vehemently denied, or to record they had bribed the soldiers who had guarded the tomb to tell a different story. Their spin on the facts was probably sufficient to satisfy any questions from the Roman authorities when news of the disappearance of Jesus' body reached them. Therefore, we would not expect much from Roman archives either.[14]

- So, the only undisputed documentation of the resurrection event is found in the New Testament record. This also makes sense given that the resurrected Jesus met only with believers. It is also consistent with the unobtrusive evidence for God that we find in the cosmos and the earth around us. People are free to take it seriously or dismiss it as they choose.

- Something very significant must have happened to transform the disciples – who huddled behind locked doors immediately after the crucifixion – into men who courageously confronted the Jewish leaders, 'turned the world upside down,'[15], toiled as servant-leaders for the rest of their lives, and were willing to die as martyrs. One of the most telling transformations was in Jesus' own brother, James. He went from being a sceptic who distanced himself from Jesus

---

14. Josephus does, but it can be argued that this was a later insertion – although it is present in all the manuscripts that have been discovered, including Arabic versions, which descend from a very early translation fork.

15. Acts 17:6

and his followers, even mocking Jesus on at least one occasion, into a pillar of the early church, seeming to become more of the 'go to' person than Peter. For me, this only makes sense if what Paul says is true: that after his resurrection, Jesus appeared in person to James.[16]

- People who argue against the resurrection being a true event usually postulate that the disciples were deceived in their grief and confusion, or wilfully fabricated a myth to preserve 'the enterprise' and their positions within it. However, lies tend to be exposed over time. If it was wishful thinking or an orchestrated lie, the number of people involved in perpetrating it was such that we could expect the wheels to fall off relatively quickly due to personal conflicts or disaffections. Or perhaps some of them would have had the moral integrity to blow the whistle at some point. The Jewish authorities would have readily documented the testimony of any whistle-blowers coming to them in this regard. They would have ensured that copies of such important documents refuting the rapidly growing Christian sect, as they called it, were distributed far and wide among Jewish communities in the then known world. If this had occurred, copies of these documents would have been preserved down through the centuries – especially given Judaism's impressive feat of having safeguarded so much of its written history. The reality is that those who postulate that Jesus' resurrection was a delusion or fabrication have no hard evidence to support their scepticism.

Many of the small, ancillary details recorded in the four gospels

16. 1 Corinthians 15:7 and its surrounding context.

of the New Testament (and in Chapter 15 of Paul's first letter to the Corinthians) are so far outside the Jewish mindset of the day that they are unlikely to have been fabricated: Jesus' body was placed in the tomb that Joseph of Arimathea, a member of the Jewish high council, had prepared for his own burial; women were the first witnesses of the resurrection; and the disciples' honest admission of their own initial unbelief (and that Jesus had chided them for this).

The New Testament goes to considerable lengths to document who Jesus is, what he was like, what he accomplished in his life on Earth, and the role he will play in future eternity. It claims very clearly that a correct understanding of Jesus is extremely important for all of us. This is not merely an academic exercise because our understanding, or lack of it, will have considerable impact on many decisions we make, and our priorities as we live our lives. Consequently, at this point of the road map you may wish to independently explore this territory more carefully and thoroughly.

Given that Jesus is the watershed between Judaism and Christianity, at some point in our road map we need to decide which of these two paths better represents the creator of the universe. Was Jesus the Messiah? Or was he an imposter? Is Judaism correct in its assessment of him, or has it missed something very significant that occurred in its own backyard? If we want to find our way home to the one who made us, then it is very important that we fully embrace God's perspective and all he has communicated through his initiatives in human history. Are the Jewish and Christian scriptures in conflict with each other, or is there a deep harmony between them? Fulfilled prophecies, what we know about Jesus, his teaching and claims, and the claims of others about him, are all factors to consider. While our thinking is taking shape, let's continue to explore some other aspects of the Bible's messages before reaching any final conclusions.

Major Bible Themes:

The Big Picture for Humankind

If the creator of the universe has communicated with humankind, then we should reasonably expect this communication to reflect the attributes of a being who is capable of creating the cosmos, earth and biosphere. The reason we are exploring the Bible in our road map, is because it reflects these attributes far more than any other source. However, we can apply an objective test to the Bible – and to any other writing that claims to be the Creator's communication to humankind. Its prophetic big picture should entail appropriately sized plans, purposes and end goals. These should be commensurate with the scale of the cosmos. They should also reflect the design and implementation ability we observe in the chemistry and systems of life, the suitability of the earth itself, and in the plethora of symbiotic networks that are essential for the biosphere to work. So, let's apply some critical thinking to the Bible's prophetic big picture.

The Old Testament prophets, who accurately predicted many aspects of Jesus' life and death, were also enabled to accurately predict specific historical events in their own generation and in their near future. Some prophets were also given insight into events at the 'end of this age', when God says he will draw this side of human history to a close, and move things on into a much greater and permanent era, lasting for the rest of eternity. The accuracy, of the prophets' fulfilled predictions of earlier events, qualifies them to be taken seriously in what they said about God's long-term plans which are yet in our future. The New Testament prophecies add further detail. In all of them, the Messiah is central to both the transition and the ensuing new order.

God's Plans for Eternity

The Bible spells out the big picture of God's plans and purposes for eternity. It states that the attributes of God's character – holiness, righteousness, justice, truth, and love – will be outworked in humankind.[1] However, God plans to do much more than cleanse and rework the current earth and scheme of things. The few Bible passages that cover this topic all indicate that both the current earth and cosmos have a use-by date, and will be discarded.[2]

Several prophecies indicate that God is working towards a completely new order that will last forever: a new heavens and new earth.[3] This suggests that the new order will probably have very different physics and chemistry that are better suited for eternity – if indeed it will even have physics and chemistry! This new order, or kingdom, will grow until it is really huge. One of Jesus' parables suggests that humans from this age will each be entrusted with servant-leadership of a number of cities in the age to come.[4] However, God's promise to Abraham about the number of his descendants[5]

---

1. Psalm 97:1-6
2. Isaiah 34:4, Matthew 24:35, Hebrews 1:11-12, 2 Peter 3:7-13, Revelation 6:14. These all suggest that the ultimate destiny of the current cosmos is a 'big crunch' that will be expedited rather than taking billions of years.
3. Psalm 102:25-28, Isaiah 65:17, 2 Peter 3:13, Revelation 21:1-4
4. Luke 19:11-27
5. Genesis 13:16, Genesis 15:5, Jeremiah 33:22

and Daniel's interpretation of King Nebuchadnezzar's dream[6] go further, and suggest that it will eventually have trillions of times more beings than the entire population of all the nations and generations in human history.[7] This is all completely unthinkable from the secular perspective of our own generation, as is the thought that God has any right to step in and interrupt the comfortable lives and societies we are busy creating for ourselves.

Yet the Bible says that this side of human history is finite, and will progress into a brief but very dark apocalyptic period that will polarise everyone, expose what their hearts are really made of, and culminate in the messianic return of Jesus. Few people seem to stop and think, beyond the straightjacket of science-fiction influenced modern expectations, about the future of humankind. Even fewer perceive the storm clouds that seem to be building on the horizon. However, when we reflect on the vastness of our current universe, we suddenly realise that the one who created it will have end goals that are commensurate with this scale, or bigger still. We also realise that he has every right to intervene and move things on, when it is wise to do so from his all-knowing perspective.

The Bible suggests the primary purpose of this current side of human history is to deal once and for all with the problem of sin. It describes this clearly as pride (which thinks itself superior to others or that it knows better than God),[8] selfishness, self-centredness,

---

6. Daniel 2

7. Since it would be a home built for eternity by an infinite God, it will probably be larger than our current universe, and may even stretch to infinity. It may even involve other dimensions.

8. Pride carries with it a blindness that is unwilling to accept that its perspective and thinking fall short of the whole truth, and need to change. In contrast, genuine humility is always ready and eager for recalibration, change, and growth. This can often be a litmus-test for discerning between the two. In reality, each one of us has a mixture of

self-absorption, self-justification, self-deception and everything else that is the antithesis of God-honouring humility, love, altruism, desire for God-aligned objective truth, and harmony with him. These self-centred and self-serving dynamics find many ways to express themselves across a wide spectrum of intensity: self-seeking, self-promotion, disharmony, insensitivity to others, indifference, unforgiveness, ingratitude, wilfulness, rebellion against God (and loving parents), unfriendliness, apathy, disrespect, contempt, slander, backstabbing, hate, hostility, violence, brutality, envy, greed, scheming, abuse of trust, theft, muggings, vandalism, self-gratification, lust, adultery, incest, perversion, rape, and many other sordid traits of humanity.

The dysfunction and evil, that flows from any of these sins, leads to a wide range of adverse consequences from distrust, through damaged and broken relationships, to the extremes of enslavement, murder, war and genocide. This self-serving sin problem must obviously be dealt with once and for all, before God can move things on to the final eternal order. All participants in the new eternal order will need to be full of humility and love. They will also need to have appreciation of, respect for, and harmony with the master-plan, lest they derail it. Who would want to see the darkness in humanity multiplied a trillion times? Who would even want to live in the perpetual hostility, fear, horror and 'star wars' of science fiction? It is interesting that God built this current earth and cosmos first, rather than something better suited for eternity from the outset. However, this displays his infinite understanding and foresight, in that God could see that the sin problem would be very real, and needed to be addressed and comprehensibly dealt with, once and

---

both in almost every aspect of our thinking, because we are not fully like God.

for all. When we reflect on this, we realise the laws of physics in the current universe are ideal for teaching us that decisions have consequences, while posing some limitation on an individual's ability to cause physical harm to numerous others.

The Greek word *euangélion* is translated as 'gospel' in modern English. It literally means good news. The first four books of the New Testament are called the gospels, since they record various aspects of the life of Jesus. The term gospel is also used to describe the Christian message as a whole. What was this new revelation that was such good news for those who penned the New Testament? It was that the infinite Creator of the universe has done what we could not do ourselves. He has taken the initiative – through Jesus' life, death and resurrection – to breathe a new spiritual dynamic into humankind. He now invites each of us into a first-hand relationship with himself that will continue for all eternity. More than this, our first-hand relationship with God will completely change who and what we are, and will prepare us for the role he wants humankind to play in future eternity. There is nothing that we can do to earn or buy this. It is so priceless, that only the generosity and enabling of God's infinite love is sufficient. All we can do is humbly accept it in the wonderfully generous spirit that it is offered, and faithfully outwork it over the rest of our earthly life and beyond.

The Bible states *very* clearly that when we die, we will all give account of our lives to God. Sadly, any person uninterested in God's initiative and plans and purposes for them, who preferred to go their own way, just cannot be allowed into the new order for eternity, because they would corrupt it. Those who responded to God in humility and allowed his plans and purposes to work in and through their lives, such that they have been authentically changed and prepared, will play an important role of servant-leadership in the new order. God will probably also use the stories and experiences they take with them – their 'knowledge of good and evil'[9] – so that new beings in the future eternity will understand the awful consequences of selfishness and sin, without having to suffer those consequences first-hand, and so that no one will ever want to go back to a world corrupted by sin.

The Bible also states clearly that this life is our only opportunity. There can be no second chance for those who have rejected God in this life, because a belated attempt to save our own skins is completely the wrong foundation. Such a response lacks integrity, is largely self-centred and tends to do the bare minimum to 'qualify', rather than aspire to the complete one hundred percent change of heart that develops from a sincere desire to please God. There would also be no conviction and courage to swim against the current of adversity that results from embracing truth, and therefore seriously inadequate preparation for the role that God wants people from this age to play in future eternity. The spiritual realities of free will are such that what Jesus achieved for us can only be embraced and appropriated in this life. Adequate preparation for our role in the age to come can be achieved only through choosing to lay down our own self-centred plans and ambitions in this life, walking instead the less popular 'narrow road.'[10] This involves seeking the authentic personal transformation that develops through opposition, trials, struggles, uncertainties and risks that are found along the journey of ever-deepening faith in God.

Reflect once more on the characteristics and capabilities of the one who created the cosmos, the nanotechnology of life, the millions of diverse life forms in the biosphere, the harmony and balance within its many ecosystems, the wonders of our human make-up,

---

9. Genesis 3:1-19
10. Matthew 7:13-14

and the rich colour and diversity within humankind. Ponder also the capabilities of an infinite being who foresees and understands the minute granularity, deft networks, and downstream effects of every human thought and interaction. When we contemplate that this current universe and earthly existence is just the overture, we realise that such a being's plans and purposes for eternity itself must be truly awesome.

The depth of perception and sheer scale of the Bible's themes, and its many prophetic claims, were far ahead of their time, and are further examples of where biblical writers seem to have had outside help.

The Transition Events

The Bible gives significant prophetic detail about the events that will occur at the end of the current epoch of human history which, it says, God will use to transition into the new order of eternity. More than half of the book of Daniel[11] and approximately 85 percent of the book of Revelation speak about these events. It was the subject of a number of the parables Jesus told during his final three-and-a-half years, when he taught and worked miracles in public. Jesus also spoke privately and at considerable length to his disciples about future events on one of the evenings in the week leading up to his arrest.[12] A number of passages in other prophetic books of the Old Testament also speak about these future events, as do various sections in most of the letters in the New Testament.

---

11. In the Jewish scriptures, written when Judah was exiled to Babylon and the surrounding region.
12. Matthew 24, Mark 13, and Luke 21 – often collectively called 'The Olivet discourse'

Some of the passages, particularly in Daniel and Revelation, use imagery that is quite difficult to understand, even from our early 21st century perspective, which is obviously two millenniums closer to the time of the end than when written. In fact, we may not be able to understand these images for governmental structures and their spiritual outworking into humankind until they actually appear on the world stage. But if the Bible is the Maker's handbook, then these passages will prove to be true. The calibre of many of the fulfilled Old Testament prophecies about Jesus would suggest these images will turn out to be extremely appropriate when eventually seen with the perspective of hindsight.

In his lengthy outline of end-time events to his disciples, Jesus predicted that there would be a great 'falling away' towards the end.[13] We can perhaps see this happening before our eyes, as our modern Western society progressively abandons its Christian heritage and values, and endeavours to build a utopia without God – little realising that self-serving and sinful human nature may not be up to that task.[14] The Bible's end-time prophecies declare that, as this trend continues, hostility towards God and persecution of Christians will increase and become ever nastier, until it reaches unbridled enmity against Jesus and his work in humankind, when the *Antichrist* appears on the world stage. The Antichrist's worldwide genocide will be on a scale that will make the Nazi Holocaust look like child's play. The followers of Jesus during the *tribulation* are called to show great faithfulness and patient endurance.[15] The enormity of the evil acts perpetrated against them will expose

---

13. Matthew 24:10-12 and 1 Timothy 4:1
14. If we want a simple example, we probably need look no further than the rapid escalation of cyber-crime over the last decade.
15. Daniel 7:25; Matthew 24:21-22; Revelation 13:5-10, 14:12-13

wickedness within modern humanity for what it is. Its sheer scale would give God huge moral high-ground (as if he needs it) to draw the curtain on this current world order, and the time would finally be right for Jesus to return and establish his messianic kingdom.

God claims that he uses fulfilled prophecy to demonstrate that he knows and controls the future, and to authenticate the biblical record as supernatural. In both the Old and New Testaments, he 'makes known the end from the beginning.'[16] God's ability to foresee deep into the future is further evidence that he is an infinite being. His knowledge of the future does not come from some magical 'time-travel' ability. It comes instead from his comprehensive understanding of every minute detail and the complex networks between them, and from his ability to foresee how all these myriads of interrelationships will play forward over time. The Bible claims, and many can testify from first-hand experience, that he fully understands our hearts. He can foresee every free choice each of us will make, and the countless other permutations that might arise from different free choices. The Bible also claims that God continually injects deft micro-influences – and sometimes major events – that help shape many attitudes and free choices for greater good in the long-term.[17]

However, prophecy also provides encouragement and hope to those with faithful hearts in the generations prior to its fulfilment. If we approach biblical prophecy aright, it will result in genuine

---

16. 'I am God, and there is none like me. I make known the end from the beginning, from ancient times, what is still to come ... What I have said, that I will bring about; what I have planned, that I will do' (Isaiah 46:9-11). This axiom is also articulated in several other passages, such as Numbers 23:19.

17. He permits 'dumb' decisions and even evil decisions, which allow humanity to learn from the consequences of their decisions when things have run their course. Regrettably, it seems that every generation – including ours – is capable of making its own dumb decisions.

heart change that takes us closer to God. Conversely, if reading and studying the prophetic passages merely tickles our fascination, and does not affect our motivation and priorities, then this would suggest that we have not read them with a humble heart.

As it was for the people who lived in the many generations of biblical history, the prophetic words of God will also be a watershed for the generation that sees the transition events. People at that time will either believe what God has spoken or dismiss it as fantasy. Those who do the latter will instead find and embrace a different story, which is more in accord with their own understanding and wishes for the future, and which requires minimal recalibration. Many of these will also become hostile towards those who believe in God, just like people described in the biblical record who persecuted and murdered the prophets of their own generation. Time itself will again prove to be the ultimate test of truth.

The sheer volume of biblical prophecy about end-time events seems quite deliberate. It has generated perspective, understanding and anticipation for every generation throughout the church age. It has inspired many great hymns and, arguably, the pinnacle of choral music, Handel's Hallelujah Chorus. However, it has also been written for the generation of which it speaks. Familiarity with and understanding of these passages instil confidence that God 'knows the end from the beginning' and can be trusted even in the darkest hours of human history.

Food for thought: Some readers may appreciate a quick side-excursion at this point. Will the origins debate contribute to the timing of the transition events?

A number of conservative voices claim that the theory of evolution has a far greater effect on the character of modern society than many people realise. However, I am not aware of many formal studies having been done to evaluate correlations between the introduction of evolution-based school curricula and crime rates, youth and adult suicide rates or other measures of dysfunction within society – and don't expect the current establishment to approve research funding for such studies anytime soon. The scientific renaissance that went hand in hand with the Reformation was championed by many who had strong Christian beliefs. Kepler's famous statement 'to think God's thoughts after him' probably best articulates the views and motivations of many prominent scientists of that period. Several generations later, the Enlightenment arguably took things into darker territory, paving the way for acceptance of Darwin's thesis. Since then *Darwinism* has been steadily shaping our society, eroding our allegiance to God and Christian values, and establishing a prevailing view that the Bible is a book of fables – that God himself, and what the Bible claims Jesus accomplished, are complete myths. The steady development of 'enlightened' perceptions and attitudes within our current societies worldwide has caused many nations to forget God[18] and selectively abandon the Christian values and thinking that created the platform for the strength and prosperity of Western civilization. This has perhaps been epitomised by recent legislative changes away from our society's traditional Christian values, and growing hostility towards those who still advocate them. Such people are often glibly or angrily dismissed, by our self-appointed political-correctness police, as being intolerant. This accelerating trend seems to be creating fertile ground for widespread acceptance of the Antichrist, were he to come soon.

If the naturalistic-origins dam were to burst, it would lead to

---

18. Psalm 9:15-20

a general change in attitudes away from evolution and its associated atheistic paradigms and back towards God and biblical values. This would reverse the decline in modern society's respect for God and in its moral character, and collective thinking would become much less conducive for acceptance of the Antichrist. However, if it became obvious that the dam was about to burst, the heart motivation that seems to drive people towards *wanting* Darwinism to be true might wilfully harden at that point, and create an even stronger readiness for human-centred propaganda from the Antichrist.

So, we could infer that the time of the end will either come before the tide turns in the origins debate, perhaps within the next couple of decades, or the pendulum will swing so that it will be at least three or four generations away. Many of the prophetic signs that are prerequisites for the time of the end have appeared in our current generation.[19] How ready is God to move things on to the final stage of human history? To what extent will modern society's general perception of origins feature in God's assessment of the best time to start the final countdown for Jesus' return? How open are we to the possibility that this might be on our watch?

Note on this and the previous section: The prophetic writings in the Bible that speak about events that are still in the future (i.e. the events building up to Jesus' return, the millennium that immediately follows this, and eternity beyond) have fascinated biblical scholars and amateurs alike over the last 2,000 years, and Jewish scholars for even longer. I am sure that you will also find the

---

19. 'Many shall run to and fro, and knowledge shall be increased' (Daniel 12:4 KJV), 2 Timothy 3:1-5a. Concerning the re-establishment of the Jewish nation: Deuteronomy 30:3-5, Jeremiah 16:14-15, 31:10, Ezekiel 37:10-14, 21-22, Ezekiel 34:13, Hosea 3:4-5, Amos 9:14-15.

subject fascinating. However, it is probably wise to avoid getting too preoccupied with prophetic details at this point in the journey. Hopefully what I have provided is sufficient for now, and gives a feel for the proportion of the Bible's prophetic content that speaks of future events (events that may be closer than we think). The Bible has many places and vistas that we can come back to later and explore in greater detail. This is what we should expect, if it has been inspired by an infinite being.

The Other Side of the Coin

This brings us to a very unpleasant topic. It is tempting to skip over this. However, if we are making an honest and balanced attempt to explore an overview of the Bible, then we should not avoid one of its significant themes. This section examines what the Bible says about those who reject God and his benevolent purposes. It complements the previous two subsections, and may provide further insights that help us better understand what the Bible claims as being God's eternal plans for us. It may also cause us to think again about some aspects of this sick world in which we live.

There are many common misunderstandings about this subject. So its treatment as part of our roadmap makes every effort to address these misunderstandings, and faithfully represent what the Bible actually says. This subsection is therefore longer than others in this part of the book. First, it lays some foundations to help understand various realities, and why God has created the solution the Bible describes. It then presents a summary of that solution, and teases it out into our adult understanding.

To begin, let's look at several things that the Bible says, both in wider contexts relevant to this topic, and directly on the topic itself:

- The Bible says that God has created humans in his own image,[20] and all of us have traits that reflect this. One facet of that image is that God is an eternal being. The Bible says there is a metaphysical component to our human make-up that will live on after our physical body dies. It calls this our *soul*. Although atheism dictates that humans cease to exist when they die, the Bible makes numerous statements to the contrary. While some who reject God may even want to be annihilated when they die, the Bible indicates that this is not possible, because it would contradict the very essence of what we are as humans, who possess an immortal spiritual dimension that transcends this physical world. The Bible says quite clearly that spiritual beings – both humans and demons – cannot be annihilated, and will live for all eternity.

- Matthew 7:7 records Jesus saying, 'Ask, and it will be given to you; seek, and you will find; knock, and it will be opened to you.' John 6:37 records him saying, '…whoever comes to me I will never cast out.' These are clear declarations of Jesus' heart (and by implication, God's heart) towards us. Like many similar statements found in both the Jewish and Christian scriptures, it seems that God intends us to take them literally, as foundational promises on which we can build our understanding.

- 1 Corinthians 13 identifies several characteristics of wise love. One of these is that it does not insist on its own way, but respects people's choices and wishes even when they do not seem to be the best option for that person. While God deeply desires that everyone he has created would relate to

---

20. Genesis 1:27

him in perfect harmony for all eternity,[21] he knows this is not realistic for those who do not want it, and that it would be completely counterproductive to force it upon them. His infinite foresight is also aware that he cannot let people like that into the new heavens and earth because they would quickly corrupt it, and spoil it for everyone else.

- Several passages state that God quietly works behind the scenes in everyone's life – even those who do not respect him.[22] If people continue to reject the opportunities God gives them in this life to see truth and change their course, there comes a point where their attitudes harden permanently in the self-serving path they have chosen. This spiritual watershed sets the clock ticking for the defining moment when, for the sake of others and the bigger picture, God will need to act in judgement against them.

- Psalm 97:2 says, 'Righteousness and justice are the foundation of his throne.' Psalm 96:10 says, 'The LORD reigns … he will judge the peoples with equity.' Galatians 6:7 (ESV) states a foundational principle of justice, 'Do not be deceived: God is not mocked, for whatever one sows, that will he also reap.' It then elaborates further (in v. 8) 'For the one who sows to his own flesh will from the flesh reap corruption, but the one who sows to the Spirit will from the Spirit reap eternal life.' In these texts, *flesh* refers to short-sighted and self-serving human nature, and *corruption* represents all that is entailed in the alternative to

21. 'The Lord is gracious and compassionate, slow to anger and rich in love. The Lord is good to all; he has compassion on all he has made' (Psalm 145:8-9).

22. 'The Lord … frustrates the ways of the wicked' (Psalm 146:9).

eternal life. The Bible clearly claims that God will judge every one of us with complete fairness and with perfect clarity. We will each reap what we have sown in this life, for the rest of eternity.

- The Bible indicates that the new heaven and earth is all about full involvement with the presence of the Father, Jesus, and the Holy Spirit; speaking with them face-to-face, and working together with them and many others in perfect harmony on various collective projects. While it will be a beautiful place aesthetically, its real beauty will be in the quality of humility, love and selfless harmony between all its participants, and much face-to-face conversation with the one who made us and loves us so deeply.

- A few incidents are recorded in the Bible where godly men caught a glimpse of the majestic holiness of God, and were completely overwhelmed and undone by it.[23] People who will make it into God's kingdom for eternity will rapturously enjoy being there only because they had embraced God's forgiveness and sought to walk the narrow road during their life on earth. This will have allowed God to reproduce himself in them as they were changed more and more into his likeness, and he will bring them into full perfection when they finally see everything clearly after 'graduation'.

- When we genuinely love someone, we want to spend time with them. One characteristic of an authentic Christian walk of faith is the growth of a deep longing for the moment

---

23. Isaiah 6:1-5, Daniel 10:4-11, Matthew 17:1-9, Revelation 1:12-18. Consider also the guards at Jesus' tomb when confronted by a being from another dimension (Matthew 28:4).

when we will meet Jesus face to face, and be brought into the presence of our heavenly Father.[24] However, for someone who has not walked that road and been changed and recalibrated deep in their being, the majestic holiness of God and finding oneself in the midst of angels and humans who are in perfect harmony with him – such that he imparts his incisive discernment to them – would be a nightmare. So too would be standing before Jesus, with an acute sense that you had ignored and squandered what he had endured on the cross for your sake also.

- The overwhelming awareness of the holiness of God, and that every thought and action – past, present and future – are utterly exposed before his infinite perception and understanding, would be completely devastating. A person with unresolved history would feel like a fish out of water. They would be highly and continually self-conscious of their own past, their current self-centred spiritual state, and that they had repeatedly rejected God's calling throughout their lifetime (when authentic change had been possible and on offer). Any desire to live there would be motivated, not by an attraction to it, but by desperation to avoid the alternative, of reaping the full consequences of the decisions they had made during their life on earth. Finally confronted with reality, the realisation that the resulting recalibration was still crassly self-centred and too little, too late, would only add to their dreadful discomfort. People who rejected or ignored God in this life would be perpetually looking for

---

24. 'Meanwhile we groan, longing to be clothed instead with our heavenly dwelling … so that what is mortal may be swallowed up by life' (2 Corinthians 5:2-4).

a place to hide. However, no such hiding places will exist in the new heavens and earth, because the Bible says clearly that this is all about being *with* God.[25,26] For them, heaven would be a living hell.[27]

- Several passages in the Bible state that justice and truth cry out for fulfilment, and ultimately *must* be fulfilled. Those who have created their own reality must be confronted with the real truth. Self-centred and self-serving delusions will be exposed for what they are. There is no neutral ground on this. We are either working towards the first-best outcomes for eternity, or against them. Justice must be done – and be seen by all to have been done. God has the task and responsibility of ensuring this occurs. There are many passages throughout both the Old and New Testaments that speak about God's pending wrath against wickedness and ungodliness. From our human experience, we often perceive anger as the outpouring of a self-centred perspective in an uncaring, unloving, and self-gratifying emotional dump. But God's wrath is something quite different. While it has much passion, this is a holy passion. God's wrath is completely objective. It is a colossal indignation on behalf of the real truth, holistic justice, and the beautiful benefits to many that could have been (and should have been) – not only in this life but, more significantly, multiplying over the course of eternity. It also stems

25. 'You make known to me the path of life; you will fill me with joy in your presence, with eternal pleasures at your right hand' (Psalm 16:11).
26. 'In my integrity you uphold me and set me in your presence for ever' (Psalm 41:12).
27. 'With you the wicked cannot dwell. The arrogant cannot stand in your presence…' (Psalm 5:4 NIV 1978).

from his accurate insight into the septic mess that each evil and self-deception would create over eternity, if he did not intervene. His moral authority as the Creator, and his ability to foresee how things will play out deep into the future, give him a mandate to ultimately confront all wilful ignorance that does not want to know or care about such things. God's wrath is outworked in definitive action, which has permanent results that leave no room for ambiguity.

- The Bible says, 'The Lord … is patient with you, not wanting anyone to perish, but everyone to come to repentance.'[28] In other passages too, it clearly states that God deeply desires the very best for each and every one of us. However, the unpleasant reality is that many people continually reject his gentle calling and the opportunities he gives them. God has given us the free will essential for authentic love. But with that comes the ability to make bad choices too.

So, God has a deep, heart-wrenching problem: What to do with the immortal beings who squandered every opportunity he gave them to engage in the process of heart-change, while they were living in the learning environment, Earth, that he had carefully crafted to facilitate such change. People who do not embrace the prerequisite process of transformation, cannot be permitted to enter the new order, and would not really want to enter it anyway. The Bible says that God's solution to this dilemma is to provide a special place for them. It calls that place *hell*. Because it was primarily 'prepared for the devil and his angels'[29] it is a spiritual rather than physical place. This will significantly limit the occupants'

---

28. 2 Peter 3:9
29. Matthew 25:41

ability to abuse one-another. Who would want to see a physical 'hell on Earth' continued forever in hell itself?

With our limited experience of only the physical world, it is difficult for us to understand something in the spiritual realm. However, the Bible gives us some insights:

- The Jewish scriptures allude to hell but do not describe it. Jesus taught about it several times, and the New Testament gives us ten images that illustrate various aspects of hell. The first five are the words of Jesus, but all ten are pretty frightening:
  - 'outside in the darkness, where there will be weeping and gnashing of teeth' (Matthew 8:12; 22:13; 25:30).
  - 'the blazing furnace, where there will be weeping and gnashing of teeth' (Matthew 13:42,50).
  - 'hell, where the worms that eat them do not die, and the fire is not quenched' (Mark 9:47-48).
  - 'the eternal fire prepared for the devil and his angels' (Matthew 25:41).
  - 'eternal punishment' (Matthew 25:46).
  - 'Blackest darkness' (2 Peter 2:17).
  - 'They will be punished with everlasting destruction and shut out from the presence of the Lord…' (2 Thessalonians 1:9).
  - 'the smoke of their torment will rise for ever and ever…' (Revelation 14:11).
  - 'the lake of fire' (Revelation 20:15; 21:8).
  - 'the Abyss' (Luke 8:31; Revelation 9:1-2; 20:1-3).

- If we merge these descriptions we get a picture of hell being on the outer, away from the light and life of God. There is much weeping, unhappiness and vexation of spirit. There seems to be a unidirectional trend of loss, of being consumed rather than building and growing, and of good things gradually being eaten away. It also is a one-way ticket. There is no second chance of being released back into the community after serving your time because, like the demons after they fell, those in hell would seem to steadily grow further from God, and worse rather than better.[30,31]

- The Bible hints that hell will need a few safeguards. Jesus' parable about the rich man and the beggar[32] says that there will be some form of spiritual barrier that will prevent its occupants from ever crossing over into the mainstream and corrupting it.

Throughout the Bible, God repeatedly claims that he always says and does what is right.[33] He has a very objective, eternal per-

---

30. In several passages, the Bible says that Satan and the demons are completely beyond redemption, and the continued nature of their activities tends to confirm this. It also says that, for humans, there is a point of no return in their spiritual attitudes and choices. However, we should be very careful not to write a person off while they still walk the earth. There have been many cases where God's grace has rescued people that others might have thought were beyond reach. A good example is the sailing ship captain and slave trader, John Newton, who later wrote the famous hymn Amazing Grace.
31. The concept of *purgatory* – a special place where people who don't immediately qualify for heaven are sent to 'pull their socks up'– is not a biblical concept. Its origins are unclear, but might be based on dubious interpretations of a couple of verses in the Old Testament. It is certainly not supported by anything that Jesus taught.
32. Luke 16:19-31
33. 'I, the Lord, speak the truth; I declare what is right' (Isaiah 45:19). These words appear in the context of an astonishing prophetic passage.

spective that will always pass the test of time. True justice requires that all-knowing perspective, which can discern whether grace and mercy will be fruitful or abused. We can extrapolate this understanding to his creation of hell, and to its being his sentence on humans whose theme song for their life was something like Frank Sinatra's hit, I Did It My Way.

The Bible does not give any detailed description about hell, except for images like those listed earlier, which suggest it is not the sort of place where a sane person would choose to spend eternity. We can be confident there will be much more to hell than we can possibly understand from our current perspective, given our minimal knowledge and experience of the spiritual world. This comment also applies to the new heavens and new earth, because the Bible does not say much about them either, beyond an infinite God creating something completely new that will be superbly fit for eternity, exceeding all we could ask or imagine.[34] We just have to accept the fact that, either way, we won't really understand much until we actually get there – whichever 'there' will apply to each of us.

One doesn't have to be particularly astute to observe that the seeds of hell are already evident here on earth. We have all experienced situations which had an awful unloving atmosphere caused by contempt, spite, hostility, intimidation, or a collision between self-serving agendas. In hell these seeds may be free to develop

---

It was written before Jerusalem was destroyed by the Babylonian king, Nebuchadnezzar, and actually names Cyrus, the king of Persia, about 100 years before his empire even gained prominence. It foretold that Cyrus would order Jerusalem and the temple to be rebuilt.

34. 'What no eye has seen, what no ear has heard, and what no human mind has conceived – the things God has prepared for those who love him' (1 Corinthians 2:9).

into full maturity, especially if God will no longer be continually working behind the scenes to keep things within limits.[35] Natural justice decrees that people should reap what they sow, including perhaps, the realisation of aspirations to build a life where God is not welcome.

God is love. But he never was, and never will be, a sugar daddy. He does not wrap us in cotton wool to shield us from the consequences of choices we make – or the consequences of procrastination when action was needed. Downstream consequences are meant to confront us with objective reality and truth, so that we can learn and change. However, it is easy to make excuses for ourselves, to blame others for the consequences, to blame God for being unfair, or plain refuse to entertain the possibility that there is any correlation between later events and our earlier choices.[36] Nothing is then learnt, nothing changes, and the downstream consequences merely serve as a just punishment – that at least some others may recognise, and learn wisdom from the example. This is another one of those seeds of hell. By contrast, humility opens the door to acknowledging and embracing truth, changing for the better, and moving towards God. Humility is a seed of heaven. Its antithesis, the arrogance that presumes that *its* perception of things is truth or puts its own spin on truth, is yet another seed of hell.

To finish off, here are a number of observations and seed thoughts that may help you further explore this biblical theme:

---

35. God seems to set short time-limits for diabolical dictators like Hitler, Idi Amin, and Pol Pot – and the Antichrist when he comes.

36. 'An oracle … concerning the sinfulness of the wicked: There is no fear of God before his eyes. For in his own eyes he flatters himself too much to detect or hate his sin' (Psalm 36:1-2 NIV 1978). This also has application to society as a whole, in norms and legislation where downstream correlations are not obvious.

- Many people think that heaven is just a more beautiful place than Earth, where you can carry on doing your own thing. They also think it is an automatic right for people who have been 'good' in this life. A number even pride themselves on following the *Golden Rule* and fulfilling Jesus' second commandment to love your neighbour as yourself.[37] They are confident this will be 'enough to see them home – if heaven actually exists, of course'. But they completely neglect Jesus' first commandment, which he said was more important: 'Love the Lord your God with all your heart, soul, mind and strength.'[38] If we genuinely love someone, we consistently want to please them. If we genuinely love God, we will try to please him by conforming to his desire for an authentic first-hand relationship with us. Jesus' first commandment is more demanding because it requires complete recalibration of one's life goals. It also unlocks a wholly new and different dynamic, which is an essential prerequisite, not only for entry into heaven, but also for the ability to enjoy it.

- The Bible says that it is not sufficient to acknowledge God from a distance. In his Sermon on the Mount Jesus said, 'Not everyone who says to me, 'Lord, Lord,' will enter the kingdom of heaven, but only the one who does the will of my Father who is in heaven.'[39] Entry into the kingdom of heaven is only through the genuine, first-hand relationship

---

37. Mark 12:31. Jesus was quoting from the laws of Moses (Leviticus 19:18).
38. Mark 12:30. Jesus was quoting Deuteronomy 6:4-5, also from the laws of Moses.
39. Matthew 7:21

that God desires, and the authentic transformation and fruit that flow from this.

- Many people measure their lives by their own self-justifying perceptions, which they presume is also the way that God will see things. However, the Bible clearly states that God is infinitely more insightful and objective. He sees not only the reality of what we are and the way we live, but also our full potential. He is also very realistic: he knows our hearts and is well able to devise practical ways to grow each individual into something much better. He can work through our lives if we desire that and ask him for it. His good plans and purposes for each of us are perfectly realistic. The Bible implies that these plans are the standard by which God will objectively judge each one of us.[40]

- Another measure God will use to judge us is how we have judged others.[41] If we have accused or been dismissive of someone for something they have said or done, but done the same ourselves, then we have condemned ourselves. If we are honest, we have all been guilty of this. The Bible says that we need to seek God's mercy and forgiveness for this, and pray for the release of his forgiveness and transforming life for people against whom we have been judgemental.[42] The principle of justice demands it, as does the one who personifies justice. People who do not seek to know and please God, do not even think in these spaces. But the Bible states that he, who will judge each one of us, surely does.[43]

---

40. Matthew 25:14-30
41. Matthew 7:1-5, especially v.2.
42. Matthew 6:14-15
43. Matthew 6:15, Romans 2:1-8

- Psalm 36:1-2 says, 'An oracle … concerning the sinfulness of the wicked: There is no fear of God before his eyes. For in his own eyes he flatters himself too much to detect or hate his sin.' We all do this. So, while God sees us with complete clarity, we usually shy away from being honest with ourselves about ugly aspects of our thoughts, words and actions. If we are not willing to be honest with ourselves in our own thinking, then we will avoid acknowledging these ugly aspects in a first-hand conversation with God that seeks his power to change us for the better. In contrast, if we really desire to please God, we will continually seek the truth and honesty that is essential for an authentic first-hand relationship with him. The accumulation of many genuine changes over the course of a lifetime results in our becoming a very different person to the one we might have been if we had pursued a self-serving and self-justifying path that never sought to please God. This is perhaps the most significant seed of hell. Whether we tend to sow this seed of dishonesty or its opposite – a seed of heaven – is the watershed that will determine our eternal destiny.

- We all tend to be caught up in the here and now of this life. This consumes many of us, and we don't regularly set aside time to nourish our spiritual life and make the ongoing decisions that affect our spiritual destiny. If we *never* do this, then the decision about our eternal destiny will ultimately be made for us.

- A common misconception of hell is typified by cartoon images of it being a torture chamber run by the devil and demons. The Bible says that Satan won't be assigned the task of running hell. He will be sent there to be on the receiving end.[44] Everyone in hell (including the demons) will probably hate him because of the lies he wilfully and maliciously told them – that they bought at the time, because they wanted to believe these more than what God said was truth.

- When we consider the seeds of hell in the world around us, we come to an awful realisation: the seeds of hell are close to home. There are many within each one of us. While awareness and personal self-discipline may reduce or even overcome some of these, they often have very subtle or deeply entrenched dynamics – including self-justification. Only the incisive power of God can truly change these dynamics. While the Bible says that God desires to do this work within each of us, it requires humility and free-will choices on our part, not only in our initial acceptance of God's perspective and purposes, but also in an ongoing daily process of change over the rest of our lives. The Bible also claims that, if we welcome him, the Spirit of God will progressively expose the individual seeds of hell he wishes to disempower and overcome, as he changes us more and more back into the image of God he originally created.
- Some people assert that God is unfair in giving people a mere seventy or so years on this earth – and for many much less – that determines their destiny for the rest of eternity. However, the Bible says the lifespan of the very early generations was much greater, in the order of 300 to 500 years. Methuselah, for example, was 969 when he died. But the

44. 'And the devil, who deceived them, was thrown into the lake of burning sulphur, where ... will be tormented day and night for ever and ever' (Revelation 20:10).

Bible also records that these generations descended into such evil[45] that God was compelled to send a worldwide flood to wipe out all but one family.[46] Taking the biblical narrative at face value, perhaps the shortened lifespans after the population bottleneck of the flood may have been one reason why God could promise that he would never send such an event again. It would seem that the current human lifespan is more than sufficient for people to make their choices. The Genesis record suggests that, beyond this, the overwhelming majority of people who have rejected God would only harden their attitudes. So, the current human lifespan allows God to achieve what is necessary from this current finite era in history, and move things on as soon as possible to the permanent end goal, which will be so much bigger and better.

- There are many unreformed criminals who were confronted with truth in the courtroom, and perhaps even saw things clearly at that time, but subsequently developed their own spin on their behaviour so that they could dismiss the truth rather than recalibrate themselves. We have all done this at times to a much lesser degree. Occupants of hell may

---

45. 'The Lord saw how great the wickedness of the human race had become on the earth, and that every inclination of the thoughts of the human heart was only evil all the time … Now the earth was corrupt in God's sight and was full of violence' (Genesis 6:5, 11).
46. If atheistic conditioning causes you to struggle with the concept of the Genesis flood, consider whether the great depths of homogenous sedimentary strata worldwide (more than a kilometre thick in places) are more consistent with a catastrophic event on that scale, or with claims that they are merely the accumulated effects of many isolated local events. This is a big subject, and one's starting assumptions usually predetermine the end conclusions.

subsequently engage in this behaviour concerning what God revealed when they stood before him to give account of their life. They would have understood the objective truth at that point, because God's deep knowledge of each of us enables him to communicate personally in a way we understand. People in hell may struggle to accept the enormous consequences of the choices they made and start looking for excuses, downplaying what actually transpired, and accusing God of being excessively strict and unfair. This propensity to flatter ourselves and twist the truth may be another reason why the Bible says that true repentance is impossible once our earthly life is over, even though God's love for us would want to facilitate restoration for everyone if there was any way to do so.[47]

- The Bible indicates that there will be no procreation in hell – which makes sense. But humans who enter heaven, will not be procreating and populating heaven either.[48] God obviously has another mechanism for its colossal growth. The Bible does not tell us how many angels are currently in heaven. One passage says that there are at least a hundred million,[49] but they may number tens or hundreds of billions. Even if it is the smaller number, such that hell starts off being more populous, it won't remain that way for long. While God's mainstream develops and grows trillions of

---

47. 'I will allow no pity or mercy or compassion to keep me from destroying them' (Jeremiah 13:14b). While God has much pity, mercy and compassion, there comes a time when he must give people over to their own self-destruction. See also Romans 1:18-32.

48. Matthew 22:30; Mark 12:25.

49. Revelation 5:11. A hundred million was the highest number in the Greek language of the day.

times bigger over the aeons, hell will remain the same size, gradually becoming a relatively tiny backwater.

- After a short while, the relative sizes of heaven and hell will be the complete opposite of the pattern on this side of history, which Jesus identified in his teaching about the broad and narrow roads.[50] This gives us an insight into God's vast perspective, wisdom and patience in that he tolerates a finite period of rebellion, because he can deftly use some aspects of this for greater long-term purposes. It also demonstrates why God must completely and permanently fix the sin problem before his new order for eternity can begin.
- One struggles to envisage an environment of continual destruction and wasting away. Perhaps the dog-eat-dog fruit of self-centredness will be free to grow to full maturity, and will play a role in hell. We gain glimpses of this dynamic when children fight, and in gang and criminal subcultures. We also see it in several festering conflicts in our own generation, where things seem to have become too entrenched to be turned around – mainly because some participants have no genuine will to seek lasting reconciliation. This is yet another seed of hell. Many of us have experienced incidents first-hand at an individual level, where this destructive dynamic has found an opportunity for expression.
- Another seed of hell is when group situations descend to the lowest common denominator. Well-meaning attempts to lift things out of this state do not gain any traction,

50. 'Enter through the narrow gate. For wide is the gate and broad is the road that leads to destruction, and many enter through it. But small is the gate and narrow the road that leads to life, and only a few find it' (Matthew 7:13-14) .

because they are not welcomed by those who are dragging it down. Probably all of us can relate one or more stories where people did the opposite of something constructive that we were suggesting, just to spite us because they did not like us, or gained some twisted pleasure from doing so.

- There are two natural tendencies within each of us that are both seeds of hell. The first is to create bubbles of flattering self-justified perception around ourselves. The second is that we gain significant pleasure from popping such bubbles in people we don't like. The collision of these two dynamics will probably create much dysfunction and vexation in hell.
- Most marriages begin with well-meant promises and great hopes for the future. Yet about half of them do not pass the tests of time. The external influences, self-centredness, insensitivity, inflexibility, and unforgiveness that creep in and ultimately destroy many marriages, are all seeds of hell. The widespread dysfunction in hell will likely creep into what were once quite beautiful family relationships and friendships in this life, and eventually destroy these too.
- Hell will probably be a very lonely place. This would stem, in part, from the loss, and eventually complete lack, of soulmates. Relief from hell's toxicity might be found by hiding away on one's own. Eternal boredom in self-imposed solitude would probably be preferable to eternal hate-filled dysfunction. However, there is another seed of hell: some people enjoy ganging up on others, and seeking them out to 'make life hell' for them.
- The images of hell the Bible gives us imply a one-way process. There is no reason for a person to expect things to improve. An awful environment, without any hope at all, is

a crushing place for the human spirit to find itself trapped. Quite literally, it would be soul-destroying.

- The Bible clearly says hell is separate from the new heavens and earth. Poetic justice may demand that it be co-located with the fiery remnants of the old earth and cosmos. A few passages in the Bible,[51] even suggest this.
- For all his infinite love and innovation, it seems that God cannot conjure up a more favourable alternative without usurping the free choice that is essential for genuine love, contradicting the essence of what it is to be fully human, or ignoring the ultimate demands of truth and justice. Even though it is so horrendous, it seems that hell is still the very best solution, when weighed against all the alternatives that God's infinite creativity can conceive.
- Jesus taught that we will each 'reap' what we have 'sown'. Those who, over the course of their lives, continually rejected God's offer to them will have run God out of options. Ultimately, they will reap reciprocal rejection from their Maker.
- Imagine a passionate, heartbroken revelation from one's Creator of what our life so easily could have been, a totally objective and incisive reprimand that exposed many sinful thoughts and actions, the sting of his holy anger towards the pride and wilfulness that chose this path instead, and then permanent rejection by him. This would in itself be a significant and deserved punishment for self-centredness, where

---

51. 'By the same word the present heavens and earth are reserved for fire, being kept for the day of judgement and destruction of the ungodly' (2 Peter 3:7).

we wasted our life chasing things that could never pass the test of time, encouraged others to do the same, influenced others away from rather than towards God, suppressed the truth about God, uttered unloving or hurtful words, and were indifferent to the needs of others. It would also be the appropriate response to two even more serious indifferences on our part: to God's infinitely good plans and purposes, and to what it cost Jesus to open the way for us to embrace them.

- However, the imagery the Bible uses, suggests that hell will be much more than time alone to contemplate our Maker's rebuke and rejection. Continually experiencing seeds of hell in their full maturity, and interacting with beings who have perfected them and gain satisfaction from paying back past offences with interest, would be deeply vexing. It would bring another dimension to Paul's warning[52] that we will reap the full harvest of seeds we have sown in this life. The Bible's imagery says clearly that hell is an awful place of perpetual torment. However, it is possible that its ongoing torment may not be caused by God, but by ever-deepening, festering, and hate-filled dysfunction between the occupants themselves.

Whatever hell is going to be like, one shudders to think of a place where love will gradually be eaten away until ultimately it is completely gone, except for distant memories of what has been lost. The same will apply to all the other God-like qualities of human character. However, there is an even more spine-chilling horror of hell: it will have to continue for all eternity – for ever and ever and ever and ever and…

---

52. Galatians 6:7-8

There is one final aspect for us to consider. We cannot possibly plumb the depths of this, but we can at least scratch its surface. It is valuable to try to understand this awful reality from God's perspective. The Bible states clearly that his infinite insight understands the uniqueness of every human individual: how wonderfully we are made, our full potential in this life and in the aeons to come, and the satisfaction we would enjoy from fulfilling this. Yet those who choose to ignore or reject this, force a very unpleasant but necessary task onto him. He must ultimately confront them with reality, and prevent them from derailing and spoiling eternity for others, by sending them to a different place – for ever. He sees the darkness and horrors of hell, and deeply desires to rescue everyone from this path. He can see how much better it would be for them, and for heaven itself, if they could be included. His love for every human individual is infinite, and he desires the very best for each of us.

Yet God's infinite love is balanced by infinite truth and wisdom, and by a holy indignation at selfishness, self-delusion, and injustice. He fully understands human nature, and knows that a deep and genuine change of heart is essential, both for the new heavens and earth to work and for humans to appreciate them. God also knows that love requires free will if there is to be a two-way expression in relationships, and that love must respect indifference or rejection if this is a person's free-will choice. His insight can see deep into the future, enabling him to be completely realistic and not cling to false hopes. Nevertheless, God's love still suffers the deep ache of rejection and unfulfillment. True love never regards those it loves with ill-will, nor does it forget them. Loving parents of wayward adult children feel this deeply and, while respecting their son's or daughter's freedom to choose, grieve over what has been lost. God understands colossal networks of deft interactions compounding over time, and can see how different choices would have played out for good over all eternity, for every individual, and for the vast collective whole. Because of this, the unfulfillment of God's love and depth of his heartache are truly infinite. And they too will continue, for all eternity…

This has been a very unpleasant and difficult section to write, and no doubt to read. The magnitude and gravity of various aspects of the last few thoughts sicken me. 'Fire and brimstone' preaching has fallen out of fashion these days. In many ways this is good, because such preaching did not give a full and balanced picture of the character and heart of God. Also fear, and the motive of saving one's own skin, are poor foundations for beginning a loving, God-centred, and mutually altruistic relationship with our Maker and heavenly Father. Hopefully this subsection has adequately addressed many common misconceptions, and faithfully communicated this aspect of the Bible's contents. It completes the full 360-degree panorama of the Bible's big picture.

Are there any hairs remaining on the back of your neck after this somewhat harrowing section? You may need to take a quick break before starting to explore the next topic, which is *much* more pleasant.

Major Bible Themes:

Messages to Us as Individuals

The Bible also speaks to us as individuals, about God's plans, purposes and principles, and it spells out very clearly how we should respond to God and live our lives, for our own greatest good.[1,2]

Its big message to each and every one of us is that God's *infinite* knowledge and insight reaches down into the minutest details of our lives. He foresees the significance of events and actions that often seem trivial to us at the time. God also knows and understands us infinitely better than we do ourselves. He understands the hurts and handicaps that every one of us suffers, the disappointments, brokenness, pride and self-deception, strengths and weaknesses – and the mitigating circumstances. He also foresees our full potential if we allow ourselves to be touched and transformed by his Spirit. Building on several prophetic passages in the Jewish scriptures, the New Testament states clearly that God has taken the initiative, through Jesus, to bring us into a first-hand

1. 'Behold, you delight in truth in the inward being, and you teach me wisdom in the secret heart' (Psalm 51:6 ESV).
2. The Bible also claims that God's infinite wisdom and planning ability is such that what is 'first-best' for each of us is also in perfect harmony with his first-best for others, and for the greater whole. We see this in the balance of Nature. In many ways, it is God's signature: myriads of details all working together for mutual good in a perfect whole. It takes colossal intelligence to achieve this.

relationship with himself. This will change our perspective of virtually everything and, over time, change our hearts and minds more and more into his likeness.

Every book within the Bible has many spiritual principles that are applicable to us as individuals, and numerous general life principles can also be learnt from it. In particular, the book of Proverbs and Jesus' Sermon on the Mount articulate many spiritual and general life principles – often with delightful succinctness.

Appendix A contains some selected verses in which the Bible speaks to us as individuals. If you are not familiar with the Bible, you may find it helpful to first read at least some of these verses, to lay a foundation for the rest of what follows in this section. The list may seem quite comprehensive, but it could easily be ten times longer.

The New Testament has many role models who genuinely lived to please God. But here are three major Old Testament characters who demonstrated what our hearts' response towards God should be.

- 'Abraham believed God, and it was counted to him as righteousness' and he was called a friend of God' (James 2:23).
- 'Teach me your ways so I may know you [God] and continue to find favour with you' (Moses speaking directly with God in Exodus 33:13).
- 'God said, 'I have found in David, son of Jesse, a man after my own heart. He will do everything I want him to do'' (Acts 13:22; 1 Samuel 13:14;).

From cover to cover, the Bible has several main themes and messages directed to us as individuals:

- Truth, and the ultimate truth – God himself – can be found only through humility. The proud and arrogant, who take it upon themselves to dictate their version of truth, do not perceive that the real truth is much bigger than they are. They do not want to know what God is like; they do not care that he has plans and purposes for them, which would lead to a better way of living that is in greater harmony with their Creator and others, and more fulfilling of their potential as human beings.

- We were born into sin: selfishness and self-centredness were our default mode from the beginning.
- Sinful words and actions, even thoughts, create flow-on effects that can pollute future attitudes and relationships. If we do not turn around, our ego-centred attempts to justify ourselves will only increase our spiritual deception.
- We are unable to free ourselves from the web of half-truths and deceit we have bought into: self-serving thoughts, attitudes and perspectives that have deviated from real truth as God defines it. Our sin and self-justification give the demonic realm a legal right to develop their hold on us, and isolate us from God and his purposes. We are not totally bound over; we remain capable of loving others and even being altruistic. However, this is usually done completely independently of God, without any understanding of how much better it would be if we partnered with him, so that God would be able to work in the situation and add another dimension. Observe our attitude if our love and generosity is treated with ingratitude, taken for granted, or if we are not recognised. Self is usually not very far away, even in the good things we do.
- God does not overwhelm us. The natural world around us

speaks quietly to those whose hearts are soft and searching for God. Nevertheless, people who do not want to know about God do not hear his voice speaking to them through creation, even though it contains many signposts. We might think that God should be more demonstrative about himself. But the way things are reflects deep wisdom and understanding of the human heart. People who do not want to know usually react badly to truth, especially when it exposes something in them that is not right. Their self-justification can sound convincing, not only to themselves, but also to others who are not discerning. Responding this way to the things of God often has eternal consequences, because we tend to build on decisions towards or away from him.[3] So, confronting us prematurely would create resistance and a hardening of our hearts, generating further opportunity for the demonic realm to keep us in spiritual self-deception, wilfulness, and blindness. If someone really does not want to know, there is no point winding them up, and giving the demonic realm a greater platform for mischief. For those of us who are not so wilful, a patient approach leaves the door open for us to come around later on, when the time is more favourable.

- When we realign ourselves with the claims and teaching of Jesus, God 'turns on the lights' and we gain insight into the spiritual dimension. However, while we are still mortal, we don't see into the spiritual realm with much clarity. It is like looking through frosted glass and seeing blurred images

---

3. Luke 7:29-30 gives a commentary on this dynamic at work during Jesus' day.

of things that are very close on the other side, but nothing at all of objects that are farther away. While this can be frustrating, the Bible says that God has purposefully made it this way, so that we can learn how to 'live by faith and not by sight.'[4] Somewhat counter-intuitively, this reduced vision fosters our first-hand relationship with God, as we learn to trust him, and later find this trust was well-founded when we look back with the advantage of hindsight. It is also very important for exposing things in our heart that God wants to change, in the development of our spiritual character, and in preparing each of us for the role that he intends redeemed humankind to play in the age to come.

- A huge part of the Christian life involves our being gradually changed, to become increasingly like Jesus, dying to our own selfishness and self-centred ambitions, and allowing God to reduce our susceptibility to pride and sin, and shape us more and more into his character. This is often a painful process, from which we easily shy away. However, once we see the quiet and genuine working of God in this way, and gradually come to enjoy the fruit and understand the downstream benefits, we begin to proactively ask God to work this way in our hearts. If you want to see first-hand answers to prayer, seek his working in this regard. It is very much in line with his plans and purposes, and there is plenty that needs to change within each of us.

- God is more interested in developing our character than any grandiose achievements, even for his kingdom. Trials,

---

4. 'For we live by faith, not by sight' (2 Corinthians 5:7), 'by faith from first to last…' (Romans 1:17), Romans 4, Hebrews 11.

struggles, and difficulties are an important part of the process by which we become an overcomer.[5]

- Balancing this struggle, however, God does want to work in specific situations and individual lives. Occasionally we have the privilege of being eye-witnesses to significant supernatural acts in answer to prayer.
- Hand in hand with this, God also wants us to be an influence for good in relationships and situations where he has placed us, so that small parts of this world will be better for our having passed through them.
- God loves us immensely. He knows how he has uniquely wired each one of us. In a number of passages, God promises that his plans and purposes for us are infinitely wise and perfect and have our greatest good at heart. God desires that we lay hold of him and his plans – and embark on a lifetime adventure.

The Bible continually esteems noble personal values – which are very different from common, self-serving, human-centred ones. It also encourages us to value the things that will pass the tests of time, rather than pursue temporary silver linings that will tarnish. The New Testament, especially, calls us into a first-hand relationship with our Maker.

Our relationship with God is a love relationship, and love requires the freedom to choose. A relationship is obviously mutual,

---

5. 'for everyone born of God overcomes the world' (1 John 5:4). 'To those who overcome, I will give the right to eat from the tree of life, which is in the paradise of God' (Revelation 2:7). 'Those who overcome will inherit all this, and I will be their God and they will be my children' (Revelation 21:7).

and requires responses and initiatives from both parties. The New Testament claims that God has already taken the initiative, through Jesus, to bring us into a relationship with himself. The beginning and blossoming of that relationship is dependent on our ongoing responses, willingness and initiatives. In the end, it is up to us. Will we lay hold, with both hands, of God's offer to us? Or will we walk away, procrastinate, or not care enough to seriously investigate his offer? The Bible says that God understands how we are wired far better than we do ourselves. He deeply desires the very best for each one of us. However, it also says it is our responsibility to choose, and he respects the choices we make.

The Maker's Handbook?

The previous sections identified some of the special characteristics of the Bible, and gave a brief overview of its content and main messages. There are two further considerations that did not fit neatly into these sections, but are worth contemplating:

- The Bible displays deep insight and timeless understanding of human nature. Many of the things it said to people and generations in history still apply two to three millennia later.
- The gospels show that Jesus had huge respect for the Old Testament writings – which were all that existed at that stage – and clearly viewed them as having been inspired by God. He continually used the phrase 'It is written,' and identified prophetic passages that spoke of him.

At this point in our road map, it is appropriate to stand back and consider the Jewish and Christian scriptures separately, and as a whole. We have looked at the unique preservation and breadth of supporting manuscripts, the supporting archaeological evidence, the number and astonishing accuracy of fulfilled prophecies, the descriptions and insight into various attributes of the Creator (that were not self-evident to the human authors at the time of writing), and the nature and extent of the Bible's contents.

If both sets of scriptures are of the same calibre and are fully consistent with each other, then it would be sensible to treat these writings as having a common source, and the Bible as a single entity. We should then carefully ask ourselves the question: Is this combined book the Maker's handbook for humankind?

If your answer to this is no, leave the door open to reviewing things in greater depth to ensure that your conclusion is correct. If you are unsure, then it may be useful to go back over some of the earlier sections and use these as a travel guide for your own additional research.

However, if your answer to this question is yes – even a tentative yes – then you have arrived at a point where you need to make another major decision: What are the implications? Am I serious in my quest and in my commitment to embrace what I discover and let it change who and what I am?

If it seems to you that the whole Bible *is* the Maker's handbook, then it will eminently serve as your road map going forward from here. However, for our closing sections, let's briefly examine where that might lead.

Where To From Here?

If you have concluded that God exists, and that the Bible is the Maker's handbook, then the way forward from this point will depend to a large extent on your background and how you are wired. If you are already reasonably familiar with the Bible, then you may be ready to make some bold decisions. However, if you are not familiar with the Bible, then it may be more 'honest before God' to be tentative until you have had the chance to read it for yourself – both to cross-check that the summary provided in the previous sections is a true representation, and to gain your own sense of its detailed content. You can refer to Appendix B for some helpful suggestions about how to approach reading the Bible. Wherever you fit in this regard, you have probably reached the point where it is time to open direct lines of communication with your Maker.

Praying is actually quite easy. God understands us and what we are thinking better than we do, and he loves us very deeply. He doesn't care if our words are clumsy, because he hears our heart more than our words. He just cares that we are being honest, with him and with ourselves. Tell him where you are at, and what you are thinking. You can then begin to read the Bible prayerfully for yourself, and embrace what God wants to say to you through it.

The importance of the Bible in a Christian's life cannot be overstated. God has provided it to anchor our first-hand relationship with him into the rock of objectivity, and into the real truth about his character, capabilities and purposes. As we diligently and regularly read the Bible, we discover many things about him, and are steadily changed in our thinking. You will develop an ever-deepening awareness of the infinite nature of God, and that he understands and loves you – and those around you – more than you ever knew. He has immensely fulfilling plans and purposes for you that are better than you could possibly imagine. His infinite intelligence has crafted his plans for you in such a way that they are not only the very best for you but also fit perfectly with his master plan, in the same way as everything in the biosphere fits together in the balance of nature for each local habitat. It takes colossal intelligence to achieve a perfect balance with such complexity. But this is easy for an infinite being. God has taken the initiative, through Jesus, to bring you into a first-hand relationship with him that also fits perfectly with the bigger picture.

If you have not done so already, somewhere along the path of your diligent reading through the Bible, you will understand God's personal invitation to you, and sense that you should respond to him. If so, do this in a way that is most appropriate for you: take a walk under the stars, or in a park or forest; sit in your favourite chair; or lie on your bed. Acknowledge where you are at, thank him for his initiative, and convey your response to him. Ask him to help you see yourself with honesty, as he sees you – the good and the bad – and to catch a sense of his potential to work for good in you and through you to others over the rest of your life and into eternity. Thank Jesus for what he endured and achieved through the cross, and receive first-hand the forgiveness and new spiritual life he released through this. Ask him to forgive your words and actions that have hurt others, for having ignored his gentle calling in the past, for any wasted years, and for times and events where you may have even worked against him. Ask God to break through the lies and twisted thinking that you have been fed over your life to date, and help you to increasingly see and recalibrate yourself according to truth. Also ask him to lead you forward from here according to his plans and purposes.

The field of aviation offers an illustration that may be useful at this point. Our life is similar to a take-off roll, except that we have no option to abort it and taxi back for another go. (Life also seems to go faster as we progress through it.) We are the aircraft, and the pilot is our own volition. The runway is our lifespan and it has a finite length. If we are not airborne before we reach the end of the runway, it is all over. The aim is to clear the boundary fence with as much height as possible, balanced with the need to achieve optimum climb speed. There is a point during the take-off roll when the aircraft reaches *rotate speed*. Every take off is unique. The rotate speed together with how far down the runway it is achieved, vary for each type of aircraft, the payload and fuel it is carrying, the altitude of the runway, and other factors like wind, temperature and humidity. Rotation is initiated by the pilot, who must pull back on the control column at that point. If he or she fails to do so, the aircraft will continue rolling, until it reaches the end of the runway, or exceeds the design limit for its tyre speed. When the pilot completes rotation, the wheels leave the ground, a completely new dimension (height) comes in to play, and the pilot gains a whole new perspective on the world. The aircraft is also in the element for which it was designed, and it fulfils its capability to fly. Finally, the end of the runway becomes a relatively insignificant milestone, because our perspective and expectations now go far beyond it.

There is something within each of us that baulks at stepping out into the unknown. We feel insecure, and perhaps even foolish. At the same time, there is also something within us that yearns for adventure. All of us fit somewhere in the spectrum between the extremes of these two traits. When Alexander Graham Bell invented the telephone, he didn't wait until he had thought through the full implications and possibilities – and designed a full telephone network for North America. He didn't continue searching for other possibilities, such as optical fibre instead of copper wires. Instead, he ran with the existing concept, and he and Thomas Watson slaved away together until they got it to work. A first-hand walk with God is very similar. We need to grab the opportunities he gives us at the time they occur. There have been many who have procrastinated at this point, and never returned to embrace his offer. A relationship with God requires appreciation of him and his invitation to us, a desire to connect authentically with our Maker, an earnestness that seizes moments of opportunity, and the courage to proactively step out into the unknown and trust him in the adventure of faith.

As a one-year-old child takes his or her first tentative steps, he or she has no idea about the big wide world and where the skill of walking will take them, or how essential it will be in their life. For most people who embark on it, the Christian journey begins in a very similar way – with faltering honest steps into the spiritual world, and into the arms of our deeply loving, heavenly Father. We have very little comprehension of where our spiritual journey will lead in this life, let alone in eternity. However, the Creator of this universe is obviously very wise and capable, and the journey of faith is one of learning to trust him with every aspect of our lives. Much of the Christian life is unspectacular and involves learning to *wait on God* for answers to prayers, and for his perfect timing. Later, when we can see with hindsight, we realise that this is the vehicle through which we continually die to our self-serving ambitions and impatience, and to the self-centred demands for instant gratification that scream at us from our 21st century world. We also realise with hindsight that these self-centred traits have been gradually exchanged for the spiritual qualities of love, faithfulness and spiritual harmony, which are all seeds and characteristics of heaven.

The Road Less Travelled

In terms of our road map, this brings us to the start of a road that not many choose to explore. It has only one, small entrance, and people who are not looking for this can completely miss it. In his Sermon on the Mount, Jesus said, 'For the gate is narrow and the way is hard that leads to life, and those who find it are few.'[1] He also said that the majority of people choose the wide and easy road instead, but warned that this leads to destruction. However, the difficult, less-travelled road, not only leads to a wonderful destination, but also provides the experiences and lessons which are essential preparation for that destination.

This final section in our road map gives a deeper understanding of the Christian life, and identifies several key aspects that are common for those who want to go deeper into God and his purposes. Many readers may not be ready for this section immediately. The other sections may have introduced a lot that is new, and you may sense that you need to have a period to read the Bible for yourself, and to cultivate your own fledgling, first-hand relationship with God. So you may wish to flag this section as something you will come back and read more fully in a few months' time. You can speed-read through it, to perhaps catch a few glimpses that could be

---

1. Matthew 7:13,14

helpful immediately. Or you might skip over it completely, and go straight to the conclusion. Other readers may wish to slow down, and read this section more carefully and contemplatively. It may trigger many thoughts of your own that go way beyond what has been written.

Embracing and cultivating our relationship with God radically changes who we are. We progressively exchange our own self-serving plans and ambitions for his altruistic, far better ones, and allow him to transform our thinking, values, character, attitudes, motivations, words and actions. We are all like icebergs. While people can see what is above the surface, most of us is below the surface and never seen by others. Most of God's private dealing with us is below the surface, and known only to him and us, and occasionally those who are very close to us. But his dealing with us at this level is an essential requirement for authenticity. Because he is an infinite being, he can foresee the fruit that will come from even the tiniest detail. In our walk with God, small changes are often the beginning of much bigger things.

In the Sermon on the Mount, Jesus said, 'for everyone who asks receives; the one who seeks finds; and to the one who knocks, the door will be opened.'[2] When we read these words, we usually assume Jesus was speaking about the way in which people come to the point of beginning a new life with God. But asking, seeking, and knocking should characterise the whole of our relationship with him. God often piques our curiosity in some way, preparing us for something new that he wants to teach us. There are many 'pearls' in his kingdom, but he doesn't give them to us if we are not ready to receive them.[3] We need to proactively cultivate our rela-

2. Matthew 7:8 and Luke 11:10
3. Matthew 7:6 (Also part of 'the sermon on the mount')

tionship with God, and deepen our appreciation of his treasures, by asking, seeking, and knocking.

Ask God to teach you the power of prayer. This permits him to work in your heart and life, and can unlock doors for him to work in situations and in the hearts and lives of others. As mentioned earlier, a great way to experience answered prayer is to ask him to expose things in our own hearts that he wants to change. God will gently, and sometimes not so gently, reveal things to us through reading the Bible first-hand or through everyday life situations that serve as a mirror and give us insight. We may make mistakes that expose self-centredness or things we need to learn. For example, if we become annoyed by the words or actions of someone else, we often find that we do the same things ourselves in some shape or form. As you then become aware of things in you that are not what they should be, take these to God in prayer, asking him to change you for the better. God is very willing to answer such a prayer request, and we find that he somehow produces a genuine heart-change over time, usually without us really understanding how he actually did so. God is very good at changing hearts! As a bonus, the accumulation of many such changes over the years increases our appreciation and enjoyment of life, and makes us a much easier person for others to live with.

The Christian journey is one of progressively being changed more and more into the likeness of Jesus which is, in turn, the very likeness of God the Father. The Bible says that Jesus was perfection personified. He had an intimate relationship with the Father, and understood his plans and purposes, and how to release them into the everyday reality of individual lives and group situations. He had immense sensitivity and love for people, and knew how to let them know they were loved, and how to lead them deeper into God. It was his love for God and for us that drove him to endure the cross. While we will never attain to that perfection, we can grow towards it, because this is God's primary purpose for each of us.

Isaiah 55:8-9, John 15:15, and 2 Corinthians 3:18 begin to come together in a beautiful three-part harmony. However, this process is an ongoing challenge because it continually confronts us with our need to change. The useful question mentioned in the early section on Telling Truth from Fiction has deep application here: When God sees things differently from us – differently from our dreams and ambitions, and even from things we have believed all our lives – *do we really want to know*? If we don't, then we risk reducing God to something we have created in our own image, which does not challenge us to change and grow. The authentic Christian walk involves loving the real, true God with all our heart, soul, mind, and strength – and embracing the all-encompassing transformation that flows from this.

As God progressively makes known his thoughts and ways first-hand, we gradually learn to view things more and more from his perspective. We learn to recognise other people's potential through God's enabling, how to genuinely love as God loves, and how to be his heart, hands, and voice to people and situations. The apostle John put it well: 'Whoever does not love, does not know God, because God is love.'[4] John then says, 'And so we know and rely on the love God has for us. God is love. Whoever lives in love, lives in God, and God in them.'[5] If we genuinely love people, we will be interested in them, and active in discovering and encouraging the gems hidden within them. We will also relish the adventure of God at work within us, which enlarges us into a person with the capacity to engage with and enjoy an ever-widening range of people. God's love is both infinitely passionate and infinitely intelligent. Learning how to love in the same manner, and to partner with

---

4. 1 John 4:8.
5. 1 John 4:16

him in this, is one of the most important ways that God changes us for the better; over time we grow to value this transformation for the precious pearl it is.

Once we nail our colours to the mast, and step out on this new adventure, we begin to perceive spiritual realities in a way that previously escaped us, and we find ourselves actively involved in the spiritual battle that rages all around us. Firstly, we become aware of the footholds into our own thinking that we previously gave to the demonic realm, and where this has borne bad fruit in our lives. While Jesus' death and resurrection has broken the power of demonic claims on us, we need to outwork that understanding ever more deeply into the details of our lives, in order to be truly free. The demonic realm will try to use these past footholds to derail us, tempt us back into sinful thoughts and actions, and spoil or destroy the new life that God is opening to us. The Christian journey involves many small episodes where God exposes streaks of self-centredness and sinful thinking in us. We need to acknowledge these things and then ask him for genuine heart-change. Ignoring issues, instead of dealing with them when we should, provides new opportunities for the demonic realm to lie to us, create self-deception, and deepen its foothold for mischief. We must take this threat very seriously. The lie 'it is just a little thing' usually marks the top of a slippery slope that develops into something more serious. If we are careless and do not embrace God's ability to set us free from these tentacles, the demonic realm will use them to deceive us and draw us into hidden traps that will suddenly destroy much good. Sadly, we don't have to look very hard before we come across people who are living examples of this. When the demonic realm springs a trap, it can cause serious and long-lasting damage – deeply hurting and crippling both us and those we love. This is not an easy matter, because demons maliciously target our weaknesses – those places where we still tolerate or justify sinful attitudes.

It is right here, in the mucky, shameful legacy of sin, that we discover the wonderful salvation of the living God, through the cleansing power of the cross and the transforming power of the resurrection. When we allow our relationship with God to become really honest, and invite him to expose and heal these ugly aspects of who and what we are, we discover that he always knows a way to empower us to make right choices in the heat of the moment.[6] We also discover that, through each of these victories, God permanently changes us to be a little bit more like him. It is also here, in the struggle with our own sinful nature, we begin to understand why God went ahead and created Satan and the demons who follow him, given that he foreknew the mayhem they would cause. It was for a much greater good: God uses them to expose weaknesses and impurities in us that he can see, but which we would not otherwise realise existed, nor understand and acknowledge. He uses Satan and the demons to create a new level of honesty, depth, and purity in our relationship with himself. These personal victories will characterise every one of us who makes it into God's mainstream for eternity. We will all have overcome the evil one through God's saving power released and outworked into our hearts.

Secondly, there is one principle God often uses in the spiritual battle. This principle flows from the reality that God has infinitely more insight and wisdom than all the demonic realm put together. It is the principle of death, burial and resurrection. God gives Satan and the demons 'enough rope to hang themselves', then deftly turns the tables, taking them (and usually us as well) by surprise. The end result is a radical, spiritual clean-out, and the growth of God's kingdom in a way that otherwise would never have been possible, and we are left amazed by God's master plan. We see this principle at

---

6. 1 Corinthians 10:11-13, 1 John 5:18

work in the lives of some of the people in the Old Testament: Noah, Abraham, Joseph, Ruth, David, Jeremiah, Daniel, and Hosea to name but a few. The principle was clearly evident in Jesus himself, and in the lives of all the apostles, especially Paul. This principle will be at work in and through us, as we seek to be changed more and more into the likeness of Jesus and to play our small part in the battle of the ages. This is where the Christian life gets tough, brutal and seemingly unfair. It is where we experience persecution and take some direct hits from incoming fire. It is where personal dreams and aspirations go onto the altar – even though they may have been good and honourable. It is where we find ourselves sitting among the ashes of seeming defeat as darkness descends on us. It is where the Spirit of God works deeply in our hearts through the long night of our personal loss, grief and anguish, and transforms our partially self-focused thinking into an attitude of accepting and trusting God's higher wisdom. It is where we discover the wonderful foreknowledge and faithfulness of our Lord and God, when the first hint of dawn starts to appear and then breaks into the full light of day. Yes, this has been worded somewhat poetically. However, there is no other way to express this, because our individual experiences of this principle at work are completely unique and personal. The principle of death, burial and resurrection operates at many different levels, as God writes his unique story through each of us. It goes against every natural instinct for comfort and avoidance of pain. This is what Jesus meant when he said, 'Whoever wants to be my disciple must deny themselves and take up their cross and follow me.'[7]

It is important to note that this principle has application far

---

7. Matthew 16:24, Mark 8:34 Jesus said this in the context of revealing his impending ordeal to his followers, several months before he was crucified.

beyond the power plays between the spiritual forces of light and darkness. It is often the way by which our own heart and character is transformed, as we progressively become less self-centred, and more in harmony with God. God also applies this principle through tragedy and other trials that are not overtly demonic, but more a product of this fallen and broken world in which we live. God has promised a day is coming when 'he will wipe every tear from our eyes.'[8] This implies we currently live in a land of tears. Reality is often different from what we would like it to be. Some difficulties are within our ability to struggle with and overcome. Many are bigger than us, requiring acceptance and recalibration on our part. As our relationship with God navigates the unexpected 'death' found in deep disappointments and shattered dreams, the Holy Spirit is somehow able to use our grief to work deep and permanent changes in our understanding and heart attitudes, that will be seeds for resurrection and the growth of God's greater purposes in our lives. The Bible states, 'in all things God works for the good of those who love him.'[9] Initially this may seem like a platitude. Then it becomes a work-in-progress. We may eventually see sufficient 'resurrection fruit' to prove the truth of this in our own lifetime. However, we won't understand the full fruit of all the tragedies and trials we suffer in this life, until we see things with full knowledge from the other side, in the presence of God. The heart changes God desires to produce through the trials of this life may bear fruit on earth, but they are also seeds for eternity that will continue to bear much fruit in the aeons to come.

Thirdly, God calls us to go on the offensive in the spiritual battle.

---

8. He will wipe every tear from their eyes. There will be no more death or mourning or crying or pain, for the old order of things has passed away. (Revelation 21:4)

9. Romans 8:28.

We gradually discover that prayer is one of our highest callings. It is a vital part of our relationship with God, and in our becoming partners with him in what he wants to do in the hearts and lives of those around us. Our prayer requests are the greatest gift that we can secretly give to our family, friends, neighbours, work colleagues and people he introduces into our network, and even to people God brings to our attention via an item on the news. Our prayers are also the greatest legacy that we can leave to our children and grandchildren. God, in his perfect timing, will work in their thinking and the circumstances of their lives, to woo them more and more into the fullness of his plans and purposes for them.

God desires intimate times with each of us; it is one of our highest privileges as God's children. We draw aside with him, listen to and understand his dreams for various people and situations, and then faithfully pray God's plans and transforming life into reality. Jesus was the one who spoke the words, 'Let there be light', and all the other 'Let there be…' statements that articulated the collective will of the triune God at the creation of the cosmos and biosphere.[10] One aspect of being changed into the likeness of Jesus, is that the triune God gives us the role of articulating their collective will and creativity into lives and situations on Earth through prayers that say in essence, 'Let there be…' The gentle chorus of prayer to God from all around the world, which he is able to hear simultaneously, must be something like the chorus of birds in all the forests on Earth.[11] It is indeed a privilege to play our own small part in this, in the confidence that aspects of eternity will be different as a result of each prayer request that articulates God's heart for people and situations. This is an area where we can often denigrate

---

10. Genesis 1, John 1:1-2, 10, Colossians 1:16-17, Hebrews 1:1-3
11. I know every bird in the mountains (Psalm 50:11)

our efforts as insufficient. But we can join with Jesus' disciples who came and asked him, 'Lord, teach us how to pray.'[12] He gave them some important lessons, and the Holy Spirit continued that work for the rest of their lives – as he will with us.

When the disciples asked Jesus to teach them how to pray, they weren't asking him for techniques to get their own 'shopping lists' filled quickly. Jesus had modelled what a genuine relationship with God looks like. The disciples recognised the role prayer played in that relationship, and this was what they were really seeking. By now you will have gained a good sense that the Christian life is all about relationship with God. (In this current 'age of the church', a significant part of our first-hand relationship is with the Holy Spirit, who comes to live within us.) In some ways, this is like the relationships we enjoy with our spouse and close friends. In others, a relationship with an infinite spiritual being is quite different. We need to learn how he speaks to us. He may speak through his written word, the Bible; through our conscience and inner thoughts; through situations and circumstances; through other people, even some who are not Christians;[13] and through the prompting and leading of the Holy Spirit, whose quiet voice we progressively learn to recognise. Gradually our centre of gravity moves from being self-centred to being God-centred, his priorities become ours, and we increasingly take on his love and other character traits as we are changed more and more into the likeness of Jesus. While we feel constrained to finish exploring his plans and purposes for this life, there is a deepening desire for the day when he says that we

---

12. Luke 11:1-13
13. While Christians may have a better understanding than most about the big picture for the future, we don't have a monopoly on all truth in the present. When our hearts are soft and eager to learn, it is amazing who God can use to articulate truth to us.

have completed his tasks at hand and can come into the fullness of his presence. There we will talk with him in complete clarity and, together with myriads of others, will enjoy him throughout his new adventure of eternity.

While the Christian life requires an ongoing relationship with God through Jesus, it is not a solo journey. God is very committed to the community of believers, the church, which is spiritual in nature, not institutional. Its members span all denominations, and even include some who are outside the established church. The true church is a movement rather than an institution. This body of believers is a living demonstration of God's love and harmony outworked among men and women, that helps people to recognise who Jesus is and the reality of God's work through him.[14] Genuine, loving Christian fellowship is another one of the special privileges that God facilitates in this life, and it will continue for all eternity. Even brief interactions with some Christians in the present are seeds for much more over the course of eternity, when there will be time to get to know them much better, and to fulfil God's plans to produce fruit and blessing through that deepening friendship. In the here-and-now of this life, Christian fellowship is essential for our own spiritual survival. The Bible refers to the church as being Christ's *body*, and says that all of us need the other parts, just as an individual part of a human body is nothing on its own and will soon die if severed from the body.[15] Sadly, a number of Christians have not understood this, and the demonic realm has been able to pick them off farther down the track.

There is a very powerful dynamic when a group of believers get together to pray, even just two or three. Although it is good and

---

14. John 17:20-26
15. 1 Corinthians 12:12-27

encouraging for its own sake, group prayer often releases God to work in lives and situations in ways that are very sovereign, which we don't usually see to the same extent when we pray alone. As you increase your Christian network, you will discover that God has been doing some amazing things under the radar. The miracle-working God of yesteryear is still the same, and doing miraculous things in our own generation. From time to time, God will give us the privilege of seeing him do exceptional things. But God also seems to enjoy working humbly in ways that are less spectacular, but nevertheless genuinely supernatural. The walk of faith in him, individually and collectively, accumulates many answers to prayer, special experiences, and true stories of God's faithfulness, trustworthiness, and power.

As we draw closer to the time of the end, we can expect that opposition will grow towards both Jesus and those who follow him. We can begin to prepare and steel ourselves for this. In due course, we may need to make some hard choices and face genocidal persecution and hardships – even in the 'Christian' Western world. Yet, in the mystery of the big picture from the perspective of eternity, trials and hardships will ultimately prove to have been the very best path for you and me. In times of trial, our character is tested and strengthened, and more seeds for eternity are planted. Our friendships and generous relationships with other Christians are often a source of mutual strength and of God's provision within those trials.

So, in tandem with seeking to develop your relationship with God, seek to develop wholesome relationships with other Christians, and to learn how God works among and through believers who comprise a local church. God's detailed plans and purposes for you will include shared journeys and adventures with other Christians. It is sensible to start connecting with any genuine Christians that you already know and respect. If you don't know any, ask God to bring one or more across your path. Do you know of a place where genuine Christians are likely to meet? Other Christians will probably be energised by the new thing that God is doing in your heart and life, and will welcome your approach. They will introduce you to other Christians and help you learn and grow in God, and some of them will become precious friends you will enjoy for all eternity. If you don't get this reaction from some, don't be discouraged: Christians come from all manner of backgrounds, and each one is on their own growth curve. God will most certainly lead you into healthy relationships with many other genuine believers who are fellow-travellers on the narrow road.

The Christian journey is one of accumulating individual and collective experiences that teach us to trust the infinite God in everything, even in the tiny details. Big doors turn on small hinges. God's thoughts and ways are infinitely higher and more insightful than ours. His way is usually not the way we would do it if we were in charge, because he sees things that we can understand only with the benefit of hindsight. A prime example of this is seen in the colossal spiritual battle that spans this age of finite history, and determines the make-up and course of eternity. The ground troops that God has chosen for this battle are ordinary, flawed and fallible mortals such as you and me, who are still learning to trust the insight, innovation and wisdom of our commander-in-chief.

Thus, the road less travelled leads to a wonderful destination, and the journey along it provides essential preparation for that destination.

Conclusion

There is a day when all the journeys and adventures of this life come to an end. That day is special. So too are all the experiences, lessons learnt, and pleasant memories we gained from the adventure. We continue to carry these with us, and they enrich and enlarge us. Many opportunities in this life are unique. Even if we revisit somewhere we have previously been, it is not the same. The timing and circumstances are different. In the same way, our own human life will one day come to an end. It will not be possible to go back and acquire experiences that we avoided or squandered when the opportunity was ripe. My grandmother would sometimes say to me, 'Life is very short, Graeme.' I am now beginning to understand what she meant.

Earlier on our road map we identified some attributes of the Creator: for example, his infinite ingenuity, planning ability and care for minute details. We found that the God of the Bible has an astonishing ability to know the future. Among the verses quoted from the Bible was 'in all things God works for the good of those who love him.'[1] God has good plans for leading us forward over the rest of our lives and beyond. However, we don't need to get overly intense about finding God's perfect blueprint for our lives. The

1. Romans 8:28

Christian life is more like sheep grazing in a paddock – it doesn't usually matter much which side of a particular rock we eat first. But there are times when it is right to move on to another paddock – and the *good shepherd* will open the gates for us at those times. Our part is to walk through God's open gates of opportunity. Much of our life is indeed like sheep grazing contentedly in their current paddock. We need to learn how to enjoy the humility of our current circumstances and to make the most of them. The heart changes and experiences that accompany our learning how to bring the fragrance of Christ into our everyday reality, prepare us for the roles that God wants us to play in more significant future situations that he foresees, both in this life and in the age to come.

Earlier, we also saw that one of the attributes of the Creator of the universe is that he seems to really enjoy diversity. Every person, town and city on the planet is unique. The uniqueness of every Christian heart and life, every Christian friendship, every local church fellowship, and every link in the huge Christian network and movement which forms the body of Christ worldwide, also reflects God's love of diversity. His gentle everyday work in people's lives illustrates his ability to understand and coordinate vast arrays of interacting details – and each detail is a seed for eternity. Along the way, we have the privilege of seeing God's genuine transforming work in our own hearts overflow to bless others, making many small parts of this world a better place for our having passed through them.

If we were created, rather than being the product of colossal chance, then the ultimate truth is the Creator himself. Surely, finding our way home to the one who made us, and learning to live more and more in harmony with his wonderful and infinitely wise purposes, has to be both *the meaning of life* and *life's greatest quest*.

Well, I trust this travel guide through some of the big questions has been helpful, as you have set aside time to think again. If so, it has been my privilege. Hopefully this book has stimulated a number of fresh thoughts of your own that go far beyond what I have written. Best wishes as you discover the road map for the rest of your life from God himself, and lay hold of the true story that he wants to write both in your heart and through you into this broken and hurting world that he still loves so deeply. By his grace and enabling at work in both of us, I look forward to meeting you at some stage and hearing your story – be that in this life or at some point early in eternity.

Appendices

Appendix A: Selected Bible verses that speak to us as individuals

Jewish Scriptures (Old Testament)

'The fear of the LORD is the beginning of wisdom, and knowledge of the Holy One is understanding' (Proverbs 9:10). Here the meaning of the word 'fear' is quite broad, and conveys a sense of awe and respect, in addition to mindfulness that God will also cause us to reap what we sow.

'Above all else, guard your heart, for everything you do flows from it' (Proverbs 4:23).

'The path of the righteous is like the morning sun, shining ever brighter till the full light of day' (Proverbs 4:18).

'In repentance and rest is your salvation, in quietness and trust is your strength … Yet the LORD longs to be gracious to you; he rises to show you compassions. For the LORD is a God of justice. Blessed are all who wait for him!' (Isaiah 30:15, 18).

Christian Scriptures (New Testament)

'Now without faith it is impossible to please God, for whoever comes to him must believe that he exists and that he rewards those who diligently search for him' (Hebrews 11:6).

'Ask and it will be given to you; seek and you will find; knock and the door will be opened to you' (Matthew 7:7).

'For God so loved the world that he gave his one and only Son, that whoever believes in him shall not perish but have eternal life' (John 3:16).

'Yet to all who did receive him, to those who believed in his name, he gave the right to become children of God – children born not of natural descent, nor of human decision or a husband's will, but born of God (John 1:12-13).

'Now this is eternal life: that they may know you, the only true God, and Jesus Christ, whom you have sent' (John 17:3).

'I am the light of the world. Whoever follows me will never walk in darkness, but will have the light of life' (Jesus speaking in John 8:12).

'So if the Son sets you free, you will be free indeed' (John 8:36).

'Because you belong to him, the power of the life-giving Spirit has freed you from the power of sin that leads to death' (Romans 8:2).

'Do not be overcome by evil, but overcome evil with good' (Romans 12:21).

'Clothe yourselves with the Lord Jesus Christ, and do not think about how to gratify the desires of the sinful nature' (Romans 13:14).

'Do not conform to the pattern of this world, but be transformed by the renewing of your mind. Then you will be able to test and approve what God's will is – his good, pleasing and perfect will' (Romans 12:2).

'[Jesus Christ], who gave himself for us to redeem us from all wickedness and to purify for himself a people that are his very own, eager to do what is good' (Titus 2:14).

'As the Father has loved me, so have I loved you. Now remain in my love … I have told you this so that my joy may be in you and that your joy may be complete. My command is this: Love each other as I have loved you.' (John 15:9,11-12).

'I am the vine; you are the branches. If you remain in me and I in you, you will bear much fruit; apart from me you can do nothing … This is to my Father's glory, that you bear much fruit, showing yourselves to be my disciples' (John 15:5,8).

'And we know that in all things God works for the good of those who love him, who have been called according to his purpose' (Romans 8:28).

'And if the Spirit of him who raised Jesus from the dead is living in you, he who raised Christ from the dead will also give life to your mortal bodies because of his Spirit who lives in you' (Romans 8:11).

'Neither death nor life, nor angels nor rulers, nor things present nor things to come, nor powers, nor height nor depth, nor anything else in all creation, will be able to separate us from the love of God in Christ Jesus our Lord' (Romans 8:38-39 ESV)

Appendix B: Some quick tips for reading the Bible

If you are not very familiar with the Bible, or haven't read it for a number of years, you might want to first read through it quite quickly to give you an overview. However, don't read it from cover to cover. Jump to one of the gospels in the New Testament first, to gain a better understanding about Jesus.

Mark's gospel is good for those who prefer something written for ordinary people, while Luke may be better for readers who have a slightly more scholarly or historical bent. John focuses more on the things that Jesus said rather than the events, although he included details about some events to set the context for Jesus' words.

Then read the other gospels, before carrying on through Acts and the rest of the New Testament. This will give you a good overview of the New Testament, and plenty of background to help you appreciate the significance of various parts of the Old Testament which you can then also read, beginning with Genesis.

Having gained an overview of the Bible, you can then begin to read it more devotionally, that is, just one or two chapters each day, praying before you start that God will give you fresh insights as you read it. It is probably sensible to read devotionally through the New Testament several times over the course of a year or so, before attempting to read devotionally through the Old Testament.

It is worth noting that Jesus introduced changes that fulfilled and superseded some of the commands that God had given to individuals who lived during Old Testament times. For instance, Jesus' death on the cross abolished the need for ritual cleansing through the temple system. It seems that God gave some of the laws of

Moses (e.g. various dietary rules) to keep citizens of the nation of Israel separate from those of the surrounding nations – preventing as many as possible from adopting their pagan worship, thinking, and lifestyles. Christian living is based on an empowering first-hand relationship with God (which is in harmony with his nature and character), rather than adherence through self-effort to a comprehensive set of rules, special days, and rituals that were necessary until Jesus' death and resurrection. It is helpful to keep this in mind when you read through the Old Testament.

Recommended Resources

Visit www.IsItTimeToThinkAgain.com for more articles and resources related to this book, including links to the web pages mentioned in the footnotes.

Acknowledgements

This book has been a part-time project spanning five years. It has been juggled alongside family life, running a business, church involvement, sports clubs, and various other commitments. Like most projects of this nature, it has not been a solo effort.

Firstly, I am grateful to my wife, sons, and daughter, both for their support and for sometimes sacrificing outings and adventures, as their husband / father spent many hours researching and writing. My wife, Mejun, also made valuable contributions both as a sounding board for many things in the book and by checking the accuracy of all the scripture references. Janelle, my daughter, spent many hours scouring the internet to find all the graphics that we have used on the cover (and many other good ones that she and I sifted through in the process).

I also owe much to Ken Francis, who was best man at my wedding. This project began as a 'personal thinking-aloud exercise', but when I was starting to wonder whether it might be useful for others, it was Ken I approached for advice and to warn me off any flight of fancy. His honest assessment and sincere encouragement set me on a course that spanned another four years, in which the original document was re-worked and expanded considerably. Ken gave many hours of his time to read through a later version of the manuscript, again making many valuable suggestions. I don't know anyone who is famous – let alone rich and famous – so when the publisher and I were discussing who could write the foreword, Ken was the one who came to mind, as he has seen the project develop from its early stages and has a special gift for crafting words.

I am also grateful to another friend, Ron Jamieson, who generously gave his time to read through the manuscript in its middle stages, and gave me helpful suggestions and encouragement. Last year, as the project entered the home straight for submitting to an editor, my sister, Sylvia, took me up on an earlier invitation to give feedback. I was not disappointed. Her sharp straight-thinking approach gave me valuable input, and her suggestions – all of which have been incorporated – far exceeded my expectations. I asked Dr Angela Meyer (PhD in horticultural science) to check the accuracy of the manuscript's scientific content, particularly the life-science aspects. She went the extra mile, giving many editorial suggestions as well. I would also like to thank two other friends, Ray Broad and Lloyd Vivian, for giving their time to independently proof-read the final book, before it went to print.

I acknowledge John Massam and the team at Castle Publishing. John has been very helpful to me as a new author, and contributed a second foreword. Castle have taken this book into a league that I could never have achieved if I had published it alone.

Lastly, but most importantly, I acknowledge the grace and enabling of our Creator and Heavenly Father for his loving patience, as he changes us for the better over the years. Those who have also been walking 'the road less travelled' for a while, will recognise that some of the observations in the second part of the book are typical of the first-hand insights we each gain from various God-orchestrated situations that expose our need to 'think again'.

Image Credits

Front cover. Earth View (NASA). Retrieved from: images.nasa.gov/details-iss038e004318.html. Galaxy NGC 1309 (NASA). Retrieved from: hubblesite.org/image/1858/gallery. Public domain.

Figure 1, page 31. Big Bang Expansion (NASA). Retrieved from: en.wikipedia.org/wiki/File:CMB_Timeline300_no_WMAP.jpg. Public domain.

Figure 2, page 32. Hubble Ultra Deep Field Image (NASA). Retrieved from: commons.wikimedia.org/w/index.php?curid=33189266. By NASA, ESA, H. Teplitz and M. Rafelski (IPAC/Caltech), A. Koekemoer (STScI), R. Windhorst (Arizona State University), and Z. Levay (STScI). Public domain.

Figure 3, page 49. Amino Acid Chirality (NASA). Retrieved from: commons.wikimedia.org/wiki/File:Chirality_with_hands.svg. Public domain.

Figure 4, page 67. DNA. Retrieved from: commons.wikimedia.org/w/index.php?curid=15027555. Used by permission of the author Zephyris (Richard Wheeler).

About the Author

Graeme Evans was born in Nelson, New Zealand in 1953, the second of four children. The family moved to Auckland in 1955, when his father joined the lecturing staff at Ardmore Teachers' Training College. Graeme had a happy childhood in the residential community at Ardmore, completing his primary and secondary schooling in Papakura. He represented Papakura High School in sports – rugby, athletics, swimming and fencing – and was also a prefect.

In 1971, he joined the Royal NZ Air Force (RNZAF) and was initially based at Wigram in Christchurch, together with other members of the 'University Squadron'. He attended Canterbury University from 1971 to 1973, graduating with a BSc in Computer Science. He and the five others who took the Stage 3 course that year may have been the very first Computer Science graduates in New Zealand. In 1974, he joined the 174 Pilots' Course, gaining his wings in April 1975. For the next seven years he flew Bristol Freighters, C-130 Hercules and helicopters out of Auckland, before being posted to a position in the Ministry of Defence in Wellington, where his computer skills were put to use and he attained the rank of Squadron Leader. Graeme left the RNZAF in 1984.

His first job in the civilian world was with the New Zealand Dairy Board, in a new section they had just established to introduce and facilitate 'end-user computing'. (IBM PCs had just come out.) After 18 months, he decided to form his own consultancy and software development company. He remained in Wellington for another two years before relocating to Auckland in 1987.

In 1994 Graeme met Mejun, originally from Taiwan, at the local church they both attended; they married in 1996. They currently live in Manukau, South Auckland, together with their two sons and daughter.

Throughout his childhood, Graeme regularly attended a Presbyterian church in Papakura with his family. Things switched into a first-hand journey in 1969, when God 'turned on the lights' for him and many others in the church youth group. The charismatic renewal had brought a fresh wind of change into many churches in New Zealand at that time. Over the decades since then, Graeme has always regularly attended a church close to where he was living – moving comfortably between various denominations – and has served in many voluntary capacities, including music, leading small groups, and eldership.

In his early years as a Christian, Graeme could see the hallmarks of design in the cosmos and biosphere, and attributed these to the God that he was experiencing first-hand. However, he held to the then-prevalent view that God had used deep-time and evolutionary processes to create the world and biosphere we have today. In 1990, a friend introduced him to several articles written by well qualified scientists, who argued against this view. Thus began a quiet journey of personal research and discovery that is still ongoing. Over the years since, Graeme has become increasingly convinced that geological strata and features display evidence that they were formed by catastrophic events rather than having accumulated slowly over millions of years. Graeme has also concluded that God did not pull the biosphere up by its bootstraps over aeons, but created various plant and animal families as originals, front-loaded with all the information necessary for subsequent speciation.

While Graeme finds much stimulation in all things scientific and engineering, his main passion is observing and participating in the way God works in people's lives – including his own.

Extras

Obedient Hearts

You were the target of dark forces
    pulling long malicious strings
Who gloated while all of heaven winced
    and hushed stillness came to angel wings
They unleashed horrific cruelty
    a scourging just the start
Yet God was working awesome Life
    through your fully obedient heart

You released a brand-new power:
    Resurrection life!
Growing grace and love, through martyrs' blood,
    and countless unsung humble lives,
Down through the generations,
    in diverse forms and parts,
God's treasure from the nations:
    A huge family…
With millions of obedient hearts

Jesus, reveal your plans through us
    with self left far behind

Write another chapter
    in your vast story of mankind
Break through demonic strangleholds
    creating many brand-new starts
Your will done on earth as in heaven
Released through obedient hearts

The above are the lyrics of a song. It has a chorus which also is a prayer:

May you grow your heart within us
Fresh hope where there's tears and pain
Living water in dry places
Father, breathe new life again
Father, breathe new life again

When Time Has Had Its Say

Some chose the path to higher ground
Others take the easy way
What's wise or dumb will be clearly seen
When time has had its say

Detailed Table of Contents

www.ingramcontent.com/pod-product-compliance
Ingram Content Group UK Ltd.
Pitfield, Milton Keynes, MK11 3LW, UK
UKHW020130250726
13967UKWH00002B/578

9 780473 465278